JOHN WAYNE'S
WILD WEST

AN ILLUSTRATED HISTORY OF COWBOYS, GUNFIGHTERS, WEAPONS, AND EQUIPMENT

John Wayne's Wild West

An Illustrated History of Cowboys, Gunfighters, Weapons, and Equipment

Bruce Wexler

Skyhorse Publishing

Copyright ©2010 Pepperbox Press Ltd.
First published in the United States in 2010 by
Skyhorse Publishing, Inc.

Skyhorse Publishing books may be purchased in
bulk at special discounts for sales promotion,
corporate gifts, fund-raising, or educational
purposes. Special editions can also be created to
specifications. For details, contact the Special
Sales Department, Skyhorse Publishing, 555
Eighth Avenue, Suite 903, New York, NY 10018 or
info@skyhorsepublishing.com.

www.skyhorsepublishing.com

10 9 8 7 6 5

Library of Congress Cataloging-in-Publication
Data is available on file.

ISBN: 978-1-62914-344-6

Printed in China

Contents

Introduction

When "Big" John Wayne steps onto the movie screen, the audience is immediately conscious of his awesome presence. He has a laconic way of talking and walking, but we sense that underneath, he is a coiled spring, ready for action. Wayne brought huge credibility to all of his movie roles, especially to his Western characters. We implicitly believe in their authenticity and their place in history. His portrayal of Davy Crockett in *The Alamo* (as Director, Wayne wanted to play the minor role of Sam Houston, but his backers insisted he take a starring role) makes us believe that we have seen the action as it happened. In reality, the Hollywood version of events sometimes ran parallel to those of real life, but not always.

The intention of this book is to celebrate John Wayne's fantastic career in Western movies, by examining the real life events, characters, and landscapes that inspired it. John Wayne's vivid portrayals bring the spirit of the West to life, making it understandable at a human level. The dusty trails are alive with camaraderie, revenge, and courage. The stockades are hotbeds of passion, betrayal, and fear. Wayne's characters stride across the Western panorama with a composure and self-confidence that perhaps no man has ever felt, but we completely believe in The Duke.

The purpose of this book is to bring a historic and cultural perspective to the West as portrayed by John Wayne. The book does this by cataloging the West itself (its kit, townscapes, cattle trails, weapons, cuisine, and characters) and by retelling the historical events that shaped the region. Archival photographs and a lively text recreate the look and feel of the Old West, through which Wayne strides forever in our imagination.

1
Guns of the Wild West

Winchester

In the opening scene of *Stagecoach* (1939) as the camera zooms into focus on John Wayne, playing outlaw Johnny Ringo, he deftly twirls in his right hand not the usual six-gun of B-movie Westerns, but a carbine. That gun was to become one of Wayne's most famous trademarks, the Winchester saddle ring carbine. The gun actually adapted for the movie was a Model 1892, which is somewhat anachronistic as the action takes place in 1880. The standard 20-inch round barrel was shortened to 18.5 inches to give easier handling and the reload action was fitted with a large loop lever so that by twirling the whole carbine the shooter could fire and reload with one hand. Wayne took this technique to its ultimate conclusion thirty years later in *True Grit* (1969) when, as Marshal Rooster Coghurn, he rode into battle against the Ned Pepper gang. With his revolver in his left hand and reins in his teeth, Rooster's right hand was free to twirl away with the carbine to devastating effect. Wayne's dexterity with this maneuver gives credit to his undoubted skill with weapons. Other movies that feature Wayne and his Winchester are *Hondo* (1953) and *The Man who shot Liberty Valance* (1962).

The Model 1892 was however just another evolution of the famed Winchester lever-action repeating rifle. The story of this iconic weapon begins back in the early Civil War era when the Henry rifle was developed. Although the Henry was later used on the frontier, developments in the Winchester models quickly overcame some of the Henry's design limitations and it became obselete. We cover this weapon as part of our Civil War chapter.

The original and archetypal Winchester carbine was the Model 1866 saddle ring carbine. Named the "Yellow Boy" after its distinctive brass frame and receiver, it is arguably one of the most distinctive looking longarms ever. The gun was a variant of the Winchester Model 1866. There was a rifle version that

Above: *Almost surreal; John Wayne as Johnny Ringo as he appears in the opening scene of* Stagecoach.

Left: *A painting by Western artist N. C. Wyeth, which depicts the era of stage robberies. Entitled "The Noble Outlaw" it reflects greatly the character played by Wayne in the movie.*

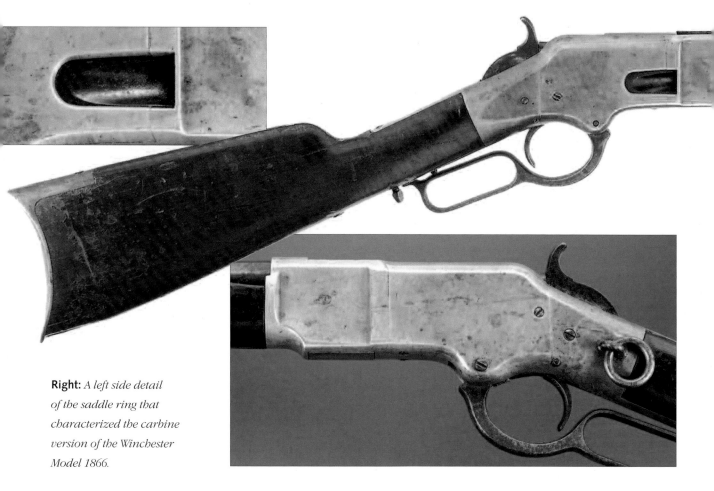

Right: *A left side detail of the saddle ring that characterized the carbine version of the Winchester Model 1866.*

had a heavier, round or octagonal barrel usually 24.4 inches in length without barrel bands and a round-barreled musket version designed for military use. This had a 27-inch barrel and looked rather ungainly as the 17-round magazine did not extend to the muzzle. The most popular version was the carbine which was ideal for handling on horseback. The saddle ring design was a hangover from the Civil War cavalry days when it could be tied to the rider's belt with a lanyard to avoid dropping while on the move. Use on the trail was very similar and this feature was retained. The 20-inch barrel of the carbine meant that its tubular magazine was necessarily shorter, holding only 13 rounds. The distinctive two barrel bands give the gun a very purposeful look as well as keeping the shorter barrel tightly located onto the forend. The lever-action (as opposed to bolt-action or other early breech loading mechanisms) made the gun easier to draw, reload, and stow away without encumbrance. Reloading was by a slot in the right side of the receiver, which allowed the shooter to reload with his right hand while keeping an eye on the action, holding the gun in his

Above: *The Model 1866 carbine was named the "Yellow Boy" for its brightly polished brass receiver. The inset detail (top left) shows the loading port in the side of the brass frame for the .44 caliber rimfire cartridges. This was the major improvement that distanced the gun from its predecessor the Henry rifle.*

Left: *A young and extremely handsome John Wayne as he appeared in* Stagecoach *in 1939. The embryonic Wayne trademarks are present here like the cavalry style tunic and Winchester carbine.*

left hand keeping it levelled ready to resume firing. Out of a total of 170,000 Model 1866s produced between 1866 and 1898 the carbine accounted for 127,000 units. All were chambered for the .44 round, either flat or pointed rimfire.

Another iconic weapon makes an appearance in *Stagecoach*–the double-barrelled side-by-side shotgun. The gun used by Sheriff Curly up on the front seat bears a strong resemblance to the Remington Model 1889, which was specially made for the Wells Fargo Company. This type of gun was ideal as its shortened barrels made it easy to draw and the fact that it fired 12-gauge shot cartridges made it a devastating weapon at close range without any great need to take careful aim. It could be fired instinctively from the hip at short notice.

Wells Fargo was one of the great institutions of the West, and was a positive force for the civilizing of the Wild Frontier. Its very name conjures a thrilling

Above: *A tense moment in the movie when Ringo and Curly stare back at the pursuing Indians. Curly's pose with his shotgun echoes that of the real life Wells Fargo guard on the facing page.*

Below: *Two views of a specially made Wells Fargo pattern padlock and key made by Ayers, Climax, and Romer.*

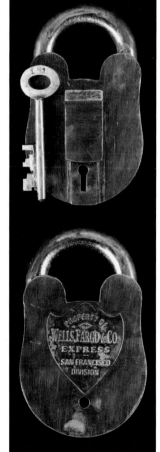

image of a six-horse stagecoach loaded with gold, thundering across the romantic plains landscape. This scene is commonplace in many of Wayne's movies. In fact, its activities became part of the fabric of the American West, serving people of every background and profession, and actively seeking to control lawlessness along the stage routes. Henry Wells and William Fargo founded the company in 1852, and the company's first office was set up in downtown San Francisco at 420 Montgomery Street, right in the heart of the tent city of the '49ers. The new company offered banking (buying gold, selling bank drafts) and express, secure carriage for all kinds of cargo, especially gold

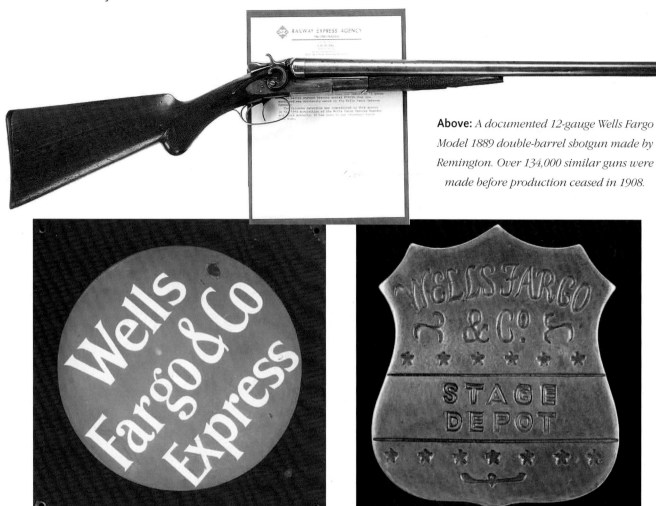

Above: *A documented 12-gauge Wells Fargo Model 1889 double-barrel shotgun made by Remington. Over 134,000 similar guns were made before production ceased in 1908.*

dust and bullion from the newly sunk mines. Right from the beginning, there was also a thread of altruism in the company culture. Wells Fargo offered their services to all "men, women or children, rich or poor, white or black." Indeed, they ran their business for all the settlers and frontiers people of the West, including blacks, whites, and Hispanics. William Wells was also an early proponent of sexual equality, later founding Wells College for Women in New York with the slogan, "Give her the opportunity!" Several women were agents by the 1880s, sometimes taking over from their husbands as company employees when they were widowed. Veterans of the U.S. Army have also worked for the company for over 150 years, helping to build the great overland stage lines and founding the financial service aspect of the company.

Integrity was a great factor in the success of the business and Wells Fargo agents often became highly respected figures in the new towns and volatile mining settlements of the West.

Above left and right: *An enamel Wells Fargo depot sign. The company also issued their operatives with a recognizable badge and their logo became a symbol of the progression of civilisation westward.*

Right: *N. C. Wyeth captured the essence of the stage era in this painting. The guard has a Winchester, which appears to be a Model 1876.*

No weapons appraisal of the West of John Wayne could be considered complete without the Peacemaker, or Single Action Army Revolver as it was more properly called. Along with the Winchester 73, the Colt Peacemaker became famous as "the gun that won the west." Both models were deliberately marketed to use the same ammunition, typically either .44/40 or .45-inch caliber. This meant that it was only necessary to carry one type of shell, a self-contained center fire cartridge. The two guns presented the all-round flexibility of a repeating rifle for long-range work, with the quick shot revolver for use at short range. Both had outstanding stopping power, provided by the large caliber ammunition.

This image of the cowboy carrying both weapons as part of his outfit was promoted by Hollywood, but the Colt was tremendously expensive at $17 (around $700 today), consequently it might not have been all that commonly used.

Above: *The classic combination of the Colt Single-action and Buscadero style Western Holster, which were both worn by Wayne during the 1930s. Note the intricate leather stitching and tooling, silver conchos, and studding that characterize this type of holster.*

But the Colt .45 Peacemaker was a familiar part of John Wayne's screen image, and when he starred in the screen version of *Hondo*, the image stuck. The gun became the model that all toy guns were based on–the author's own nickel-plated die-cast version was a personal childhood favorite–as it was with countless millions of other kids that grew up in the golden age of Westerns.

Ironically, the gun was not the direct result of Samuel Colt's own design, as he died in 1862. This was before the advent of the type of metal cased center-fire ammunition that made the 1873 revolver so effective. But it can certainly be argued that Colt's powerful vision for revolving firearms propelled the company forward for many years after his death. After all, as the popular saying went, "God made man, but Colonel Colt made them equal."

The featured example was the property of the Sheriff of Magdalena New Mexico. It has its original handmade single loop holster, decorated with brass tacks and braided rawhide edging. Many guns of this type have been handed down in families for generations.

Gun belts and Holsters

All through the 1930s, in his B-movie stage, John Wayne packed a Colt Single Action in a Buscadero style holster.

The Buscadero rig is a gun belt and holster, developed in the early 1900s for Texas lawmen, consisting of a curved belt with one or two slotted side panels, and a holster suspended from the slot. (Buscadero is from a Spanish word meaning "seeker" or "searcher"–usually applied to lawmen.)The belt and holster are often highly decorative with tooled leather, fancy stitching, silver conchos, and metal studding. For a faster draw a leather thong at the base of the holster could be tied to the gunfighter's leg to avoid the holster binding on the gun. Because early Western movies often used real-life cowboys as actors the rig they were wearing was copied by the stars as they came along. The flashy style

Below: *A serious gunslinger's leather shoulder holster made by Heiser. This could be used to keep a weapon concealed beneath a gambler's fancy coat.*

Above and below: *Western belts became very ornate during this period. Studs and leather tooling as well as bullet loops were the order of the day as these antique examples show.*

Above: *A fine example of a Buscadero rig with hand tooled leather and a silver buckle.*

Right: *The Buscadero holster shown on the previous page without the gun covering it. The loop at the top will allow it to be worn on quite a thick belt; this arrangement is known as a Mexican loop.*

of the Buscadero rather suited the "dude ranch" image that Hollywood purveyed at the time. Later Western movies such as the Spaghetti Westerns relied on a far more realistic and plain approach to leatherware. This was known as the "Walk and Draw," an angled-forward holster that incorporated a metal plate to stiffen the holster and lessen the internal friction when the gun was withdrawn. The gun was secured by a loop over the hammer. This pattern featured heavily on TV Westerns of the period. Other types illustrated are the California or Slim Jim pattern and the Mexican Loop.

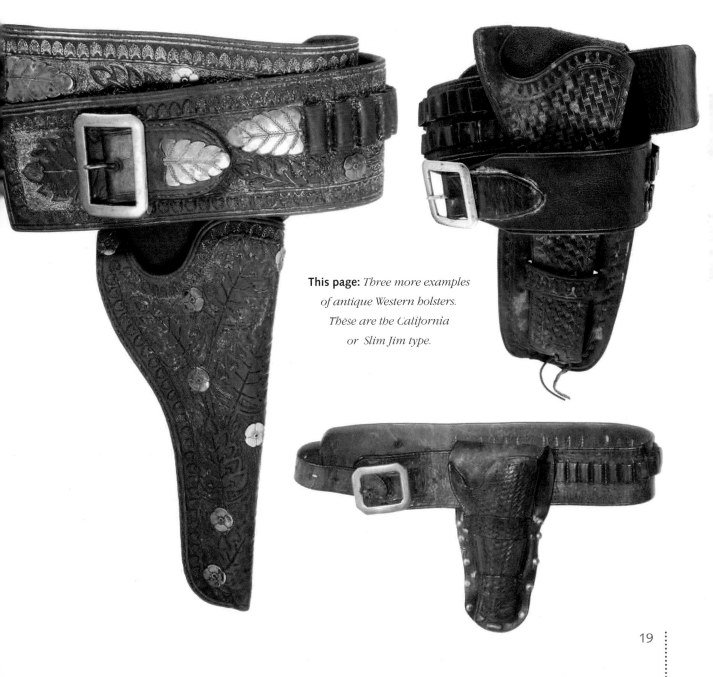

This page: *Three more examples of antique Western holsters. These are the California or Slim Jim type.*

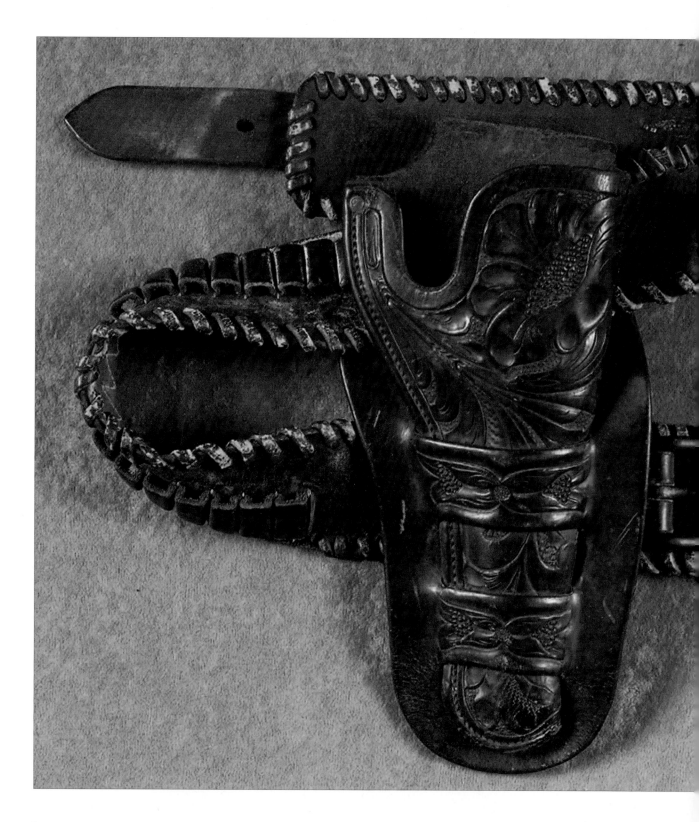

Left: *A more plain Slim Jim style holster and belt such as a cowboy might wear for everyday use on the trail.*

Below: *A Western belt that doubles as a money belt– the belt has a lining compartment where a hand could keep his wages safe away from prying eyes.*

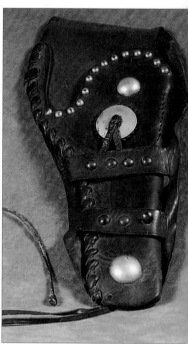

Left and below left: *A plain belt that doubles as a cartridge belt. A deep studded belt with doubled-decker style silver buckles and two very heavily decorated holsters.*

Below: *A holster with every possible kind of adornment. It has two brass-studded loops, a silver concho with a thong, two large mother-of-pearl studs, and a leather thong to tie it to the users leg. Many of these additional decorations could have been added by a competent amateur along the trail.*

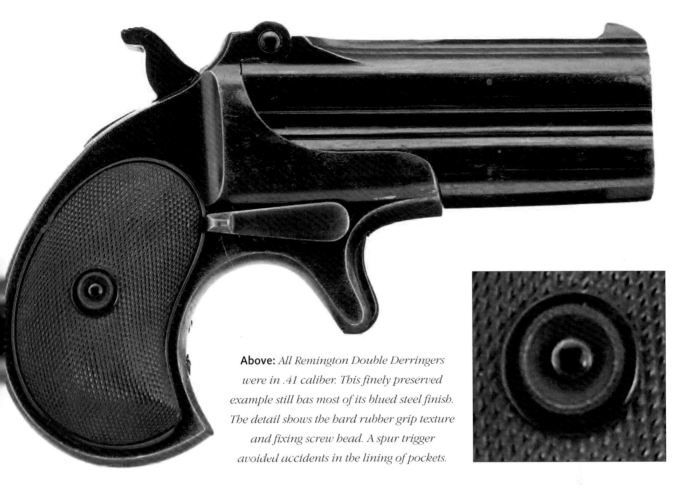

Above: *All Remington Double Derringers were in .41 caliber. This finely preserved example still has most of its blued steel finish. The detail shows the hard rubber grip texture and fixing screw head. A spur trigger avoided accidents in the lining of pockets.*

The Shootist

Wayne's last movie about an aging gunfighter dying of rectal cancer featured a rich variety of gunslingers' weapons. John Wayne as J. B. Books, the gunfighter, uses a concealed Remington Double derringer in the opening stages of the film. Anyone in a "last-ditch" situation wanted to be sure that he or she would have as many opportunities as possible to repel an attack. Most multi-barrel derringers were either complicated or large and heavy (or both), but the compact Remington twin-barrel version seemed to offer a compromise. Thus, these Remington "over-and-under" derringers were popular and were manufactured, with minor variations, from 1866 to as late as 1935, during which time some 150,000 were completed. All known versions were in .41 caliber, but in a variety of finishes, such as blued steel, nickel, and even silver plated.

The Colt Single Action Peacemaker is used by several characters in the movie; J. B. Books himself and saloon rat Jack Pulford (played by Hugh O'Brian who was best known for his starring role in the ABC television series *The Life and Legend of Wyatt Earp*). The model used was the Civilian Model or Quick

Draw, which had a 4.75-inch barrel, one favored by gunfighters as the shorter barrel would clear the holster quicker.

The Great Western revolver is also used in the film. These Single Action Army Replicas, made in the '50s, were the revolvers used by John Wayne in the film. They were a set of two engraved revolvers presented to him by the now defunct Great Western arms company. It is also thought that because Wayne would not have had his personal guns tampered with (most studio guns were adapted for safety reasons), he was probably the only person on the set using live ammunition. According to the well known gun-writer John Taffin, the revolver that is thrown through the saloon by Gilliam Rogers (Ron Howard), is not one of Wayne's Great Westerns, but a movie prop, made using a Ruger Blackhawk, modified to look like a Colt. Colt themselves had ceased production of the model just before the outbreak of WWII, which caused a number of companies to produce their own version including Ruger and Great Western. However when Colt reintroduced the gun in 1955 this caused some of the new companies to struggle and fade out.

Jack Pulford carries a Smith & Wesson No.3 break-top revolver with a six-inch barrel. Jack's gun in the film was a nickel-plated example, but the more common form of the gun was, as illustrated here, the Smith & Wesson No. 3 model Army revolvers nicknamed "Russians." The guns got their nomenclature as they were part of a massive order from the Russian authorities, which absorbed Smith & Wesson's entire manufacturing capacity for a full five years.

Below: *This .44 special caliber Colt Single-action Army revolver with a 4.75-inch barrel and holster was used by the legendary Arvo Ojala to teach shooting and fast draws to movie stars like John Wayne and Clint Eastwood. The handgun certainly appeared in movies and it has been improved to look good on camera by varnishing the grips and rebluing the metal parts.*

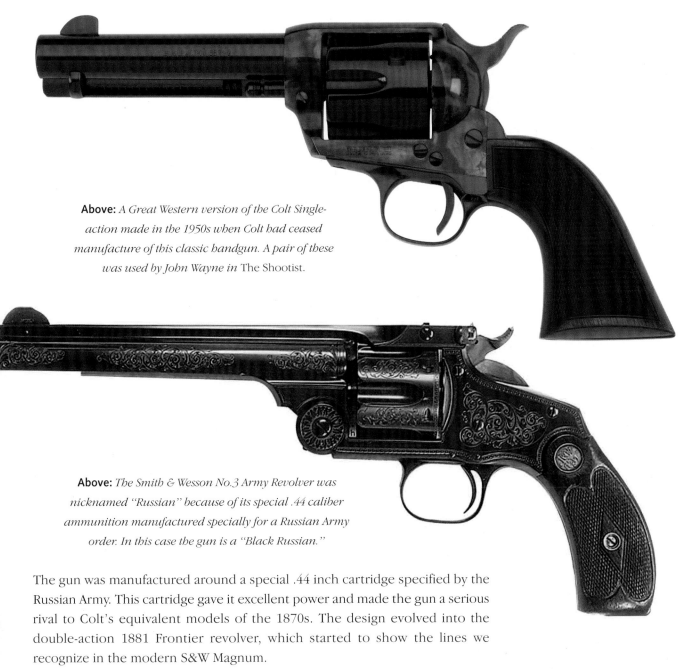

Above: *A Great Western version of the Colt Single-action made in the 1950s when Colt had ceased manufacture of this classic handgun. A pair of these was used by John Wayne in* The Shootist.

Above: *The Smith & Wesson No.3 Army Revolver was nicknamed "Russian" because of its special .44 caliber ammunition manufactured specially for a Russian Army order. In this case the gun is a "Black Russian."*

The gun was manufactured around a special .44 inch cartridge specified by the Russian Army. This cartridge gave it excellent power and made the gun a serious rival to Colt's equivalent models of the 1870s. The design evolved into the double-action 1881 Frontier revolver, which started to show the lines we recognize in the modern S&W Magnum.

The No. 3 model remained in production for many years. This example has been engraved after leaving the factory. This was not unusual. The dark blue/black case-hardened finish of the barrel cylinder and frame contrasts beautifully with the engraving, which is filled in with gilt to set it off. It is both fancy and deadly at the same time. A brace of these revolvers in a pair of holsters were serious equipment for the Western gunfighter.

Left: *John Wayne as Rooster Cogburn steadies the cumbersome Colt Dragoon on the shoulder of Kim Darby as Mattie Ross in a memorable scene from* True Grit.

True Grit

In *True Grit* Wayne plays opposite Kim Darby as Mattie Ross who is seeking her father's murderer in Indian territory (modern day Oklahoma). She is armed with an ancient and cumbersome Colt Dragoon which she can barely hold.

The Colt Walker revolver (also known as the Whitneyville-Walker or Colt Model 1847) was designed for use by the Army's U.S. Mounted Rifles (USMR), which were also known by their European name of "Dragoons." The Walker was a six-shot, .44 caliber weapon with a 9-inch barrel and an overall length of 15.5 inches, which weighed no less than 4 pounds, 9 ounces. This, plus problems of unreliability, led to the development of the Colt Dragoon, or Model 1848, of which some 20,000 were produced for government service between 1848 and 1860, with more made for sale on the civilian market. All Colt Dragoons carried six .44 caliber rounds in an unfluted cylinder, many of which were engraved with battles scenes and marked "U.S. DRAGOONS." It was a single-action revolver, with a 7.5-inch barrel and an overall length of 14 inches; weight was brought down to 4 pounds. It was very robust, with the barrel keyed to the chamber axis pin and supported by a solid lug keyed to the lower frame.

Above: *The Colt Dragoon came in three models, 1st, 2nd, and 3rd. The detail identifies this gun as the 1st Model because it has round cylinder notches. Both later models had rectangular notches. The 3rd model differs in having a fully rounded trigger guard where the 1st and 2nd models had squared back guards.*

Guns of the Wild West

The fallout from the Civil War had a significant impact on the development of the Western Frontier. Many men, who had learned the use of weapons in five years of bitter conflict, were now turned loose to colonize the new territories.

Gun design and technology had developed rapidly in the Civil War years. Troops, who had begun the conflict with muzzle-loading, single-shot weapons, had ended up armed with repeating, breech-loading arms. These very weapons were in the hands of both the lawmen and the lawless. This made the West a volatile place and launched a particularly violent period in American history. The image portrayed by John Wayne and Hollywood may have made it seem that every Westerner was uniformly equipped with a Colt revolver and a Winchester rifle, but the reality was very different. The products of both these makers were expensive. The Colt Peacemaker of 1873 cost $17, which was a whole chunk of a month's wages for the average cowhand. A more affordable handgun would have been an army-issue Colt Navy, a Whitney, or a Remington. The Frontier was flooded with pistols like these in the post-War period. The same rationale was true for rifles. The new Winchester 1866 "Yellow Boy" carbine cost $40, which was equivalent to a whole month's wages for most men on the Frontier. An ex-Union Army Spencer Model 1860 was a far more sensible option. Concealed weapons, such as pocket pistols and derringers, also became popular with many Westerners, particularly gamblers.

Of course, it could be argued that the right gun could save your life in the unstable West, and was a good investment. But many were forced to arm themselves as best they could.

The pages that follow examines a wide variety of interesting weapons that saw action on the Frontier, particularly in the wild years between 1860 and the end of the century.

Above and top left: *This Colt Dragoon 1st Model is in particularly fine condition and it is possible to see the customary engraving of a battle scene on the cylinder. A 4-pound weapon would have been a difficult gun for a young girl to control and the fact that it is her dead father's weapon with which she plans to avenge him is one of the dramatic elements of the film.*

Colt Revolvers

Samuel Colt's revolvers had proved popular in the Mexican War, as the government had wisely placed an order (instigated by Samuel Walker), for Colt's monster Model 1847, also known as the Colt Dragoon, or Colt Walker. Right from the start, Samuel Colt understood the significance of his guns to the Western market. Scenes of Dragoons fighting Indians, and other western combat, were engraved on the cylinders to illustrate this connection. Colt's percussion revolvers fought through the Civil War, and the post-War period. In 1873, the Single Action "Peacemaker" (as the gun was nicknamed) replaced these weapons. Along with the Winchester 1873 rifle, the Peacemaker can truthfully be said to have been one of the weapons "that won the West." Other handguns made appearances at gunfights, stage hold-ups, gambling dens, and along the dusty trails. But no other pistol eclipsed the reputation of the Colt.

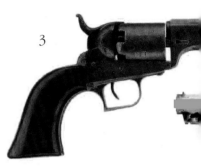

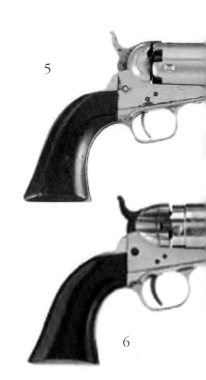

1 First Model Dragoon made in 1848. This gun had a six-shot cylinder in .44 caliber, a 7½-inch barrel, and weighed a massive 4 pounds, 9 ounces.

2 Third Model Dragoon, identified by its rounded trigger guard and 8-inch barrel. 10,000 of these weapons were made between 1851 and 1860.

3 Model 1848 Baby Dragoon. This was made for the civilian market, which demanded lighter, less cumbersome weapons. It was a 5-shot .31-caliber weapon with optional barrel lengths. This one has a 5-inch barrel.

4 Model 1849 Pocket Revolver, which replaced the Baby Dragoon. Over 325,000 of this type were made between 1850 and 1873. The gun was available with 3-, 4-, 5-, or 6-inch barrels. This example has the popular 4-inch barrel.

5 Model 1849 Pocket Revolver in nickel finish, also with a 4-inch barrel. Both examples carry the address "Saml. Colt, New York City."

6 Model 1849 with Cartridge conversion. One of many examples of the model that were either new builds, or conversions, this gun has a new round barrel with no ejector, and is fitted with a new rebated cylinder, chambered for .38 centerfire cartridges. This gun remained in manufacture until 1880.

7 Colt Model 1849 Wells Fargo. This gun was a special order of weapons for the Wells Fargo company, designed to provide backup firepower for coach guards once they had used up their two shotgun rounds.

8 Model Navy 1851. This is an example of one of the most popular handguns ever made and is easily identified by its octagonal barrel. Over 215,000 were made between 1850 and 1873. The term "Navy" was eventually used to classify any revolver of .36 caliber. Many fighting men preferred the lighter weight of the Navy to other, heavier weapons. This model was available both for military and civilian order procurement.

9 Model 1860 Army. This was the .44 caliber equivalent of the "Navy." Designed to replace the Third Model Dragoon, over 127,000 of the total production run of 200,000 guns were procured by the U.S. Government. The gun weighed 2.74 pounds and had a 7.5- or 8-inch barrel.

10 Model 1861 Navy. This gun is distinguished by its rounded-off barrel and trigger guard. Over 39,000 examples of the weapon were produced.

continued

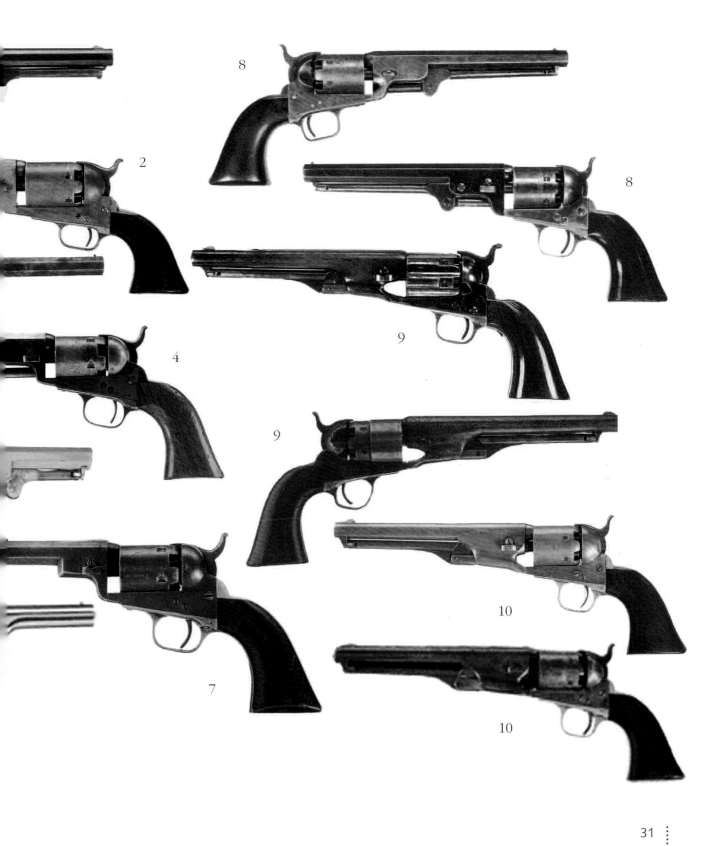

8

2

8

9

4

9

7

10

10

11 The Colt-Richards. The conversion involved removing the ramming lever, turning off the rear of the cylinder, and adding a conversion plate to take rimmed cartridges, which were loaded and removed from the rear. This is a converted Model 1860 Army revolver.

12 Model 1862 Police revolver in .36 caliber. Over 28,000 examples of this model were made between 1861 and 1873. Many were employed as civilian weapons. This example has a 5½-inch barrel, and a 5-round fluted cylinder.

13 Model 1873 Single Action. Another gun credited with being the "gun that won the West." It shared its .45 caliber with the Winchester 1873, and used the same ammunition. This meant that an individual only needed to carry a single type of cartridge in his saddlebag or belt. This example is heavily engraved by specialist engraver L. D. Nimschke. It also has added pearl grips.

14 The Colt-Thuer Conversion. This conversion enabled Colt to circumvent the Rollin White patent on bored-through cylinders. The patent didn't expire until 1869. However, the conversion was a rather cumbersome affair, as the cartridges were still loaded and removed from the front.

15 Colt Storekeeper was a cut-down, lighter caliber version of the Lightening Model, which was developed for self-defence and easy concealment. It had a 3.5-inch barrel, and was .38 caliber.

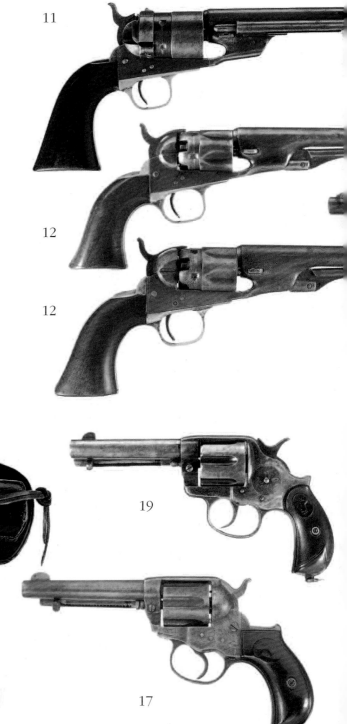

11

12

12

16

19

17

17

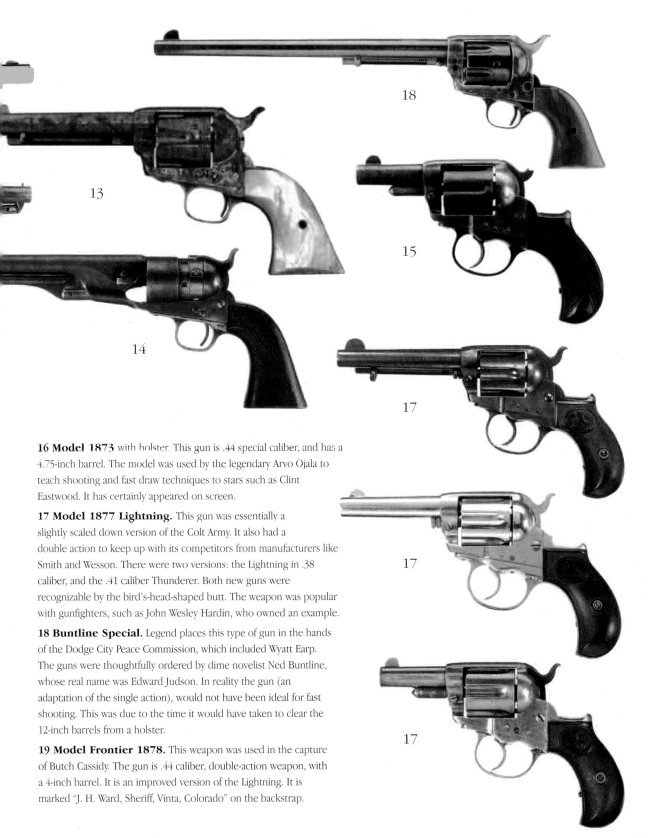

16 Model 1873 with holster. This gun is .44 special caliber, and has a 4.75-inch barrel. The model was used by the legendary Arvo Ojala to teach shooting and fast draw techniques to stars such as Clint Eastwood. It has certainly appeared on screen.

17 Model 1877 Lightning. This gun was essentially a slightly scaled down version of the Colt Army. It also had a double action to keep up with its competitors from manufacturers like Smith and Wesson. There were two versions: the Lightning in .38 caliber, and the .41 caliber Thunderer. Both new guns were recognizable by the bird's-head-shaped butt. The weapon was popular with gunfighters, such as John Wesley Hardin, who owned an example.

18 Buntline Special. Legend places this type of gun in the hands of the Dodge City Peace Commission, which included Wyatt Earp. The guns were thoughtfully ordered by dime novelist Ned Buntline, whose real name was Edward Judson. In reality the gun (an adaptation of the single action), would not have been ideal for fast shooting. This was due to the time it would have taken to clear the 12-inch barrels from a holster.

19 Model Frontier 1878. This weapon was used in the capture of Butch Cassidy. The gun is .44 caliber, double-action weapon, with a 4-inch barrel. It is an improved version of the Lightning. It is marked "J. H. Ward, Sheriff, Vinta, Colorado" on the backstrap.

Colt's Competitors

1 Beaumont Adams percussion revolver. Thousands of these guns were imported into the United States during the Civil War, by both sides. The gun was advanced for its time, being self-cocking. This gave the user double-action quick-fire in a fight at close-quarters. This example is in .44 caliber, with a 6-inch barrel.

2 Brooklyn Bridge Colt Copy. This is a classic example of the many copies that were made of the Colt Pocket models. It even has a battle engraving on the cylinder.

3 Cooper Pocket Revolver is one of around 15,000 made at the company's Philadelphia factory in the 1860s. An early double-action, .31 caliber gun, it would have been useful as a self-protection weapon.

4 Hopkins & Allen XL Double Action. This was one of a large number of budget priced revolvers marketed with names like Captain Jack and Mountain Eagle. They were five-shot, solid-frame weapons, produced in a variety of calibres. This gun is .32.

5 Manhattan Navy. The Manhattan Arms Company was one of many manufacturers who began to manufacture Colt-style revolvers once Colt's patent expired. The guns were well made and over 80,000 were produced. Colt took legal action to try to prevent their production.

6 Marlin XXX 1872 Revolver. John Marlin, a former employee of Colt, began revolver production when Rollin White's patent expired in 1869. Some 27,000 of this .30 caliber, center-fire revolver were produced between 1872 and 1877.

7 Metropolitan Navy. This gun was manufactured in 1864, when the Colt factory was damaged by fire. The Metropolitan models were almost indistinguishable from the Colt originals of the time.

8 Nepperhan Revolver. This was manufactured during the Civil War as a copy of the .31 caliber Colt. Over 5,000 were made.

9 Remington Model 1861 Army. This was a solid, reliable, and popular weapon. Many thousands were made during the Civil War. Afterwards, they were available for use on the Frontier.

10 Remington Model 1861 Navy. This gun was referred to as the "Old Model Navy." It followed the same design as the Army version but in .36 caliber. Thousands also saw wartime service.

11 Remington Army Model 1875. This was Remington's answer to the Colt Model 1873. It was a single-action gun, produced in .44 and .45 calibers. The weapon never really challenged the Colt, but Remington always had its supporters.

12 Remington New Model Police Revolver. This was Remington's response to the plethora of Colt Police and Pocket revolvers. It had a single-action arm in .36 caliber, and a 3-inch barrel. It was a compact, concealable weapon that could pack a hefty punch.

continued

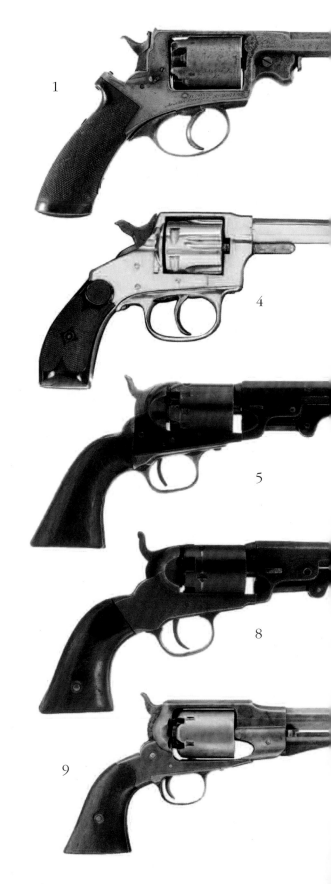

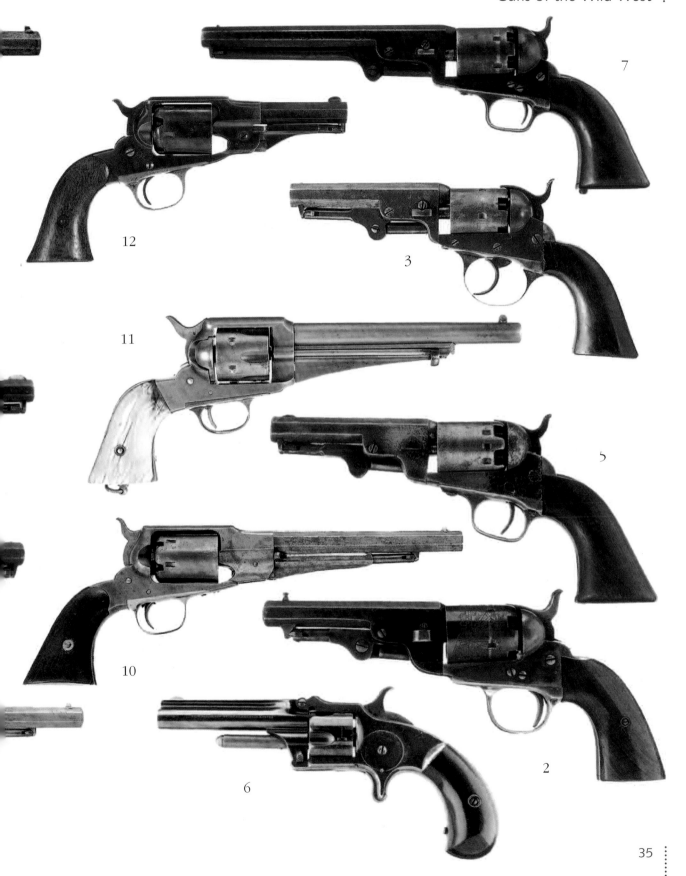

7

12

3

11

5

10

2

6

13 Remington Conversion Revolver. This gun is an example of one of the many revolvers that were converted to fire cartridge ammunition when the Rollin White patent expired in 1869. This is a New Model Pocket Revolver in .38 caliber.

14 Smith & Wesson Model 2 Army Revolver. This was available at the beginning of the Civil War and was an immediate success as it fired rimfire cartridges. Over 77,000 examples were sold between 1861 and 1874.

15 Smith & Wesson Model 3 Schofield. This gun was developed by Major George Schofield, as a heavy cavalry revolver. It was ordered by the government in 1875. However, due to the pre-eminence of the Colt Single Action, stocks were sold off in 1887. The majority found their way to the Western Frontier, and many fell into the hands of outlaws, such as Frank and Jesse James and Bill Tilghman.

16 Smith & Wesson Model 3 Russian. The gun got its name from a large order that Colt received from the Russian Army for a gun that could use a special .44 caliber Russian "necked" cartridge. These guns also made their way into the domestic market.

17 Spiller & Burr revolver. This was one of the products of the CSA armory in Macon, Georgia, during the Civil War. It was based on the Whitney 1858 Navy Revolver but due to the chronic lack of materials in the South, it was made from brass and iron, rather than steel. This example appears to have has made its way West, with the addition of brass studs on the handgrips. These were a hallmark of Indian ownership.

18 Starr Army Revolver Model 1863. Over 32,000 of this single-action revolver were produced between 1863 and 1865. The gun had an 8-inch barrel and fired a .44 rimfire cartridge.

19 Starr Model 1858 Navy Revolver. This is a double-action revolver in .36 caliber. It has a 6-inch barrel.

20 Whitney Navy Revolver. Over 33,000 of this popular revolver were made. Unlike the Colt, the Whitney had a solid frame with an integral top strap above the cylinder. This made it stronger and more robust in service. Many survived to see action on the Frontier.

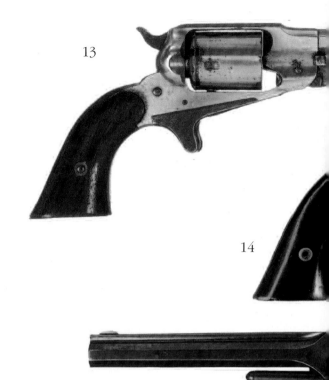

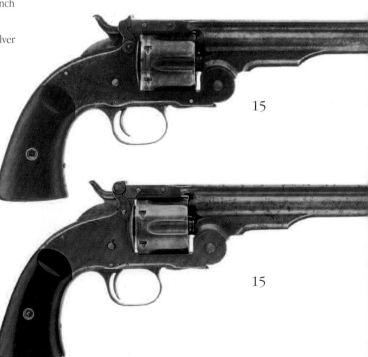

17

18

16

19

20

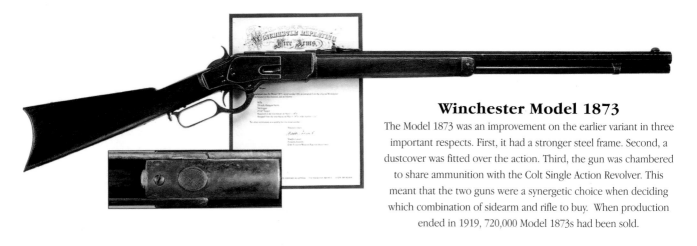

Winchester Model 1873

The Model 1873 was an improvement on the earlier variant in three important respects. First, it had a stronger steel frame. Second, a dustcover was fitted over the action. Third, the gun was chambered to share ammunition with the Colt Single Action Revolver. This meant that the two guns were a synergetic choice when deciding which combination of sidearm and rifle to buy. When production ended in 1919, 720,000 Model 1873s had been sold.

Model 1873 Sporting Rifle

This model has a 24-inch octagonal barrel and is the "Third Model" variant, which has an integral central guide for the dust cover.

Model 1873 with a 24-inch round barrel.

Model 1873 Carbine fitted with a saddle ring
and a 20-inch round barrel with two bands.

Model 1873 Trapper's Carbine

This has a shortened 16.25-inch round barrel.

Model 1876

The Model 1876 incorporated changes necessitated by the more powerful cartridges that were coming into use. It had a larger more robust receiver. The sporting rifle version shown here had a 28-inch round barrel together with a correspondingly longer forend.

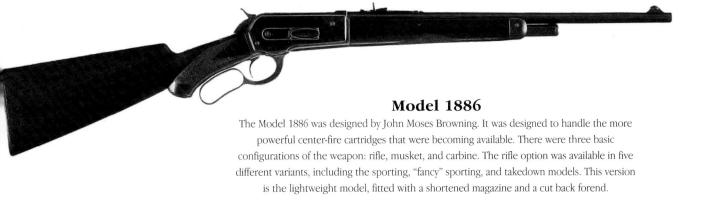

Model 1886

The Model 1886 was designed by John Moses Browning. It was designed to handle the more powerful center-fire cartridges that were becoming available. There were three basic configurations of the weapon: rifle, musket, and carbine. The rifle option was available in five different variants, including the sporting, "fancy" sporting, and takedown models. This version is the lightweight model, fitted with a shortened magazine and a cut back forend.

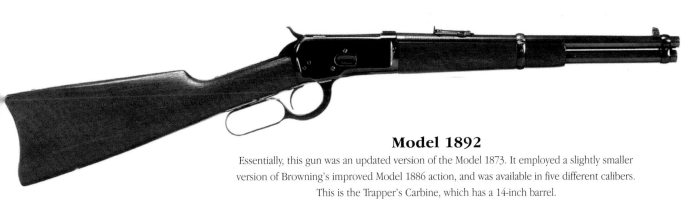

Model 1892

Essentially, this gun was an updated version of the Model 1873. It employed a slightly smaller version of Browning's improved Model 1886 action, and was available in five different calibers. This is the Trapper's Carbine, which has a 14-inch barrel.

Model 1894

This gun used the first of the smokeless powder cartridges. Although the days of the traditional West were drawing to a close, working cowboys and villains were still keen to exploit the latest weapons technology. The Wild Bunch was still operating when this gun was released.

Model 1885

The Winchester Model 1885 used the first patent that the company bought from John M. Browning. It was the first single-shot rifle to be manufactured by the company. Winchester manufactured 139,000 of these weapons between 1885 and 1920. There were two variants: the "High Wall" and "Low Wall." The difference was defined by the angle of the frame where it covers the hammer. On the Low Wall version, the frame leaves the hammer and breech visible. On the High Wall version, only the spur of the hammer is visible.

Model 1890

This Winchester model was also designed by the Browning Brothers. It was the company's first-ever slide-action rifle. It achieved great popularity, selling over 775,000 units. The gun was a late entry in the story of the West, but was a great little hunting gun for the trail.

Model 1895

John Browning's Model 1895 was the first Winchester lever-action rifle to feature a box magazine. In this case, it was non-detachable, and held five rounds. The gun received the highest possible endorsement when it was adopted by Theodore Roosevelt as his favorite hunting rifle.

Spencer

Christopher M. Spencer was born in 1841. Initially, he made his weapons at South Manchester, Connecticut, but moved to Boston in 1862. Spencer's range of repeating rifles (equipped with 7-shot magazines) made a real difference to Union forces during the Civil War. Immediately after that conflict, the U.S. Army used Spencers in the Indian Wars. Foolishly, a revised gun was issued to the troops, fitted with a device known as the Stabler cutoff. This converted the Spencer to a single shot weapon. It was erroneously believed that soldiers would aim more carefully if they only had one shot. It is also likely that the revised version was designed to save money, as it was felt that repeating weapons squandered ammunition. Spencer went out of business in 1869 as the profits of the successful war years dwindled.

Model 1860 Repeating Carbine

Personally endorsed by President Lincoln after he witnessed a field trial, this gun was one of the most charismatic weapons of the Civil War. After the war, it was widely available for civilian use. The gun fired a .52 caliber rimfire straight copper cartridge.

Model 1860 Rifle

This rifle was similar to the carbine, but had a longer, 30-inch barrel, which was fully stocked, almost to the muzzle. The stock was fitted with an iron forend cap, and three barrel-bands.

Model 1865 Carbine

This later model of the Spencer carbine had a shorter 20-inch barrel, and was chambered for .50 cartridge, which had been adapted for use in the Indian Wars. The lighter but more powerful 56-50 cartridge improved the gun's ballistic performance. In a close fight, like that at Beecher's Island, repeating rifles were hard to beat. They were also prized by Westerners as a handy saddle gun.

Spencer Sporting Rifle

After the Civil War, Spencer produced weapons for the civilian market. This hunting rifle is chambered for .45 caliber ammunition, and has a 32-inch barrel. Many of these guns were adapted for Western use by gunsmiths in Denver and San Francisco. This one has been altered by A. J. Plate of San Francisco.

Western Shotguns

The shotgun is ideal for close-range defense and offense, and was used by lawmen and outlaws alike. Shotguns are usually loaded with lead pellets or buckshot, and are fired from the hip. This results in terrible devastation at short range, without the need for taking careful aim. They were used by Wells Fargo guards, sheriffs, and bank robbers as well as homesteaders and ranchers.

ROPER. SPO
HART

Parker Shotgun

Charles Parker's sons took over his company in 1868. They recognized the peacetime
need for shotguns, and designed this classic side-by-side shotgun with external
hammers. Many owners had the barrels of their Parker shotgun shortened.

Roper Revolving Shotgun

After the Civil War, the Roper Sporting Arms Company designed a revolving shotgun.
It was equipped with four steel cartridges, which could be reloaded with shot and
powder. These were fitted into a cylindrical housing. Colt produced a similar
revolving shotgun, based on the design of their revolving rifle.

Winchester Model 1887 Lever Action Shotgun

This Browning-designed gun was sold with either a 30- or 32-inch barrel, in either 10- or 12-gauge. The five-
shot magazine was housed in a tube under the barrel. A Riot version was also available, with a 20-inch barrel.
The Model was a favorite with the Texas Rangers.

Other Western Rifles

As the century wore on, new technology overtook some of the earlier of weapons that dated from the Civil War. All guns were now breech-loading, and ammunition was more sophisticated and powerful. Specialist gunsmiths adapted guns to customer's preferences, and a huge range of sporting, target, and hunting rifles was offered to a growing market.

Remington No. 1 Sporting Rifle

This gun employed Remington's famous Rolling Block action. It has a 28-inch barrel
chambered for .44 caliber center fire cartridges.

Colt Revolving Carbine

This gun was patented on September 10, 1855, and was available in various calibers, including .36,
.44, and .56. It also came in various barrel lengths, ranging from 15 to 24 inches

Marlin Model 1881

This is Marlin's first lever-action rifle; 20,000 were sold on the western frontier. This
example is made in .40-60 caliber, and has a 24-inch octagonal barrel. Marlin
remains a name in the lever action market to this day.

Deringers and Vest Guns

As the West progressed, a new breed of men arrived. Clad in tailored jackets and dust-free Derby hats, the gamblers had hit town. Unlike the cowboys, these men did not wear large Colts holstered in plain view, preferring to hide small, but deadly, short-barreled guns about their person. These were often concealed in a vest pocket, inside a hatband, or in a well-tailored sleeve. Guns like these settled many an accusation of cheating. Guns like these were also popular with saloon girls, and more respectable ladies. They were ideal for self-defense, and could be concealed in a purse or a garter. Here is a selection of these weapons of concealment.

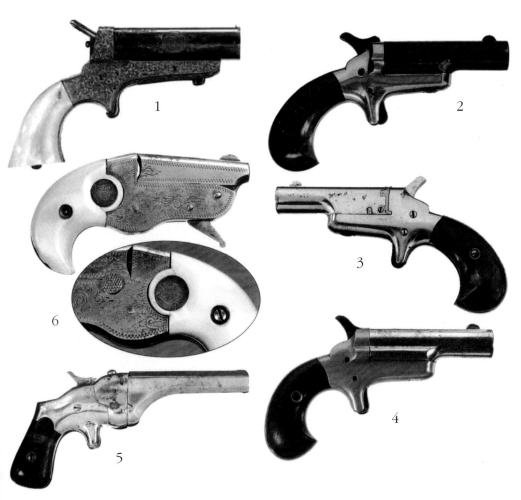

1 Tipping & Lawden 4-barrel pistol. Four barrels are better than one. Master Gunsmiths Tipping & Lawden of Birmingham, England, manufactured this Sharps design. It was then imported into the United States. The gun has 3-inch barrels and is .31 caliber. It is lavishly decorated with much engraving and pearl grips.

2, 3, 4 Colt Deringers. These are three examples of the Colt Third Model Deringer. The gun was designed by Alexander Thuer, and was often known as the "Thuer Derringer." All three examples are .41 caliber weapons with 2½-inch barrels. The barrels pivoted to one side for loading.

5 Hammond Bulldog. This is a crudely finished single-shot self-defense weapon of .44 caliber. Nevertheless, it would be effective at close range. It has a 4-inch barrel and must have kicked like a mule!

6 Hopkins & Allen Vest Pocket Deringer. This cleverly camouflaged trinket was just 1¾ inches long, and fired a .22 caliber round. It could (literally) fit in the palm of the shooter's hand and remain concealed until the last moment.

7 National No. 2 Deringer. Moore's Patent Firearm Company was established in Brooklyn in the mid-nineteenth century. The company changed its name to The National Arms Company in 1866. This gun is the No. 2 Model. It has a spur trigger, and is loaded by dropping the barrel down to one side. Following the takeover of the company by Colt in 1870, this design was marketed as the Colt No. 2 Deringer.

8 Remington Elliot Ring Trigger Pistol. This pistol relied on four solid static barrels to deliver four shots. It was chambered for .32 caliber ammunition. The ring trigger was pushed forward to rotate the firing pin, then pulled back to cock the mechanism and fire.

9 Remington No. 2 Vest Pocket Pistol. Designed by Joseph Rider, this .32 caliber vest pocket pistol fired a single shot. It was equipped with the unique Rider split-breech loading system, and had a 3¼-inch barrel.

10 Remington Double Deringer. This was the ultimate design for last ditch defense. The over-and-under barrel layout was less cumbersome and heavy than that of multi-barrel guns. The gun was also reliable, and fired two rounds in .41 caliber: an assailant-stopping load. The gun became extremely popular and over 150,000 were manufactured between 1866 and 1935.

11 Sharps pepperbox. Strictly speaking, this design by master gunsmith Christian Sharps is a multi-barreled pistol rather than a pepperbox. Nonetheless, the gun became a very popular weapon. The gun was reloaded by sliding the barrel block forward along a rail to access the breech. The four-barrel system was static and the firing pin rotated to fire each chamber in turn.

12 Wheeler Double Deringer. This weapon was designed and manufactured by the American Arms Company. It features two vertically-mounted barrels that were rotated manually. This example has a 3-inch barrel block, chambered for two .32 caliber rounds. It has a nickel-plated frame, a spur trigger, and blued barrels.

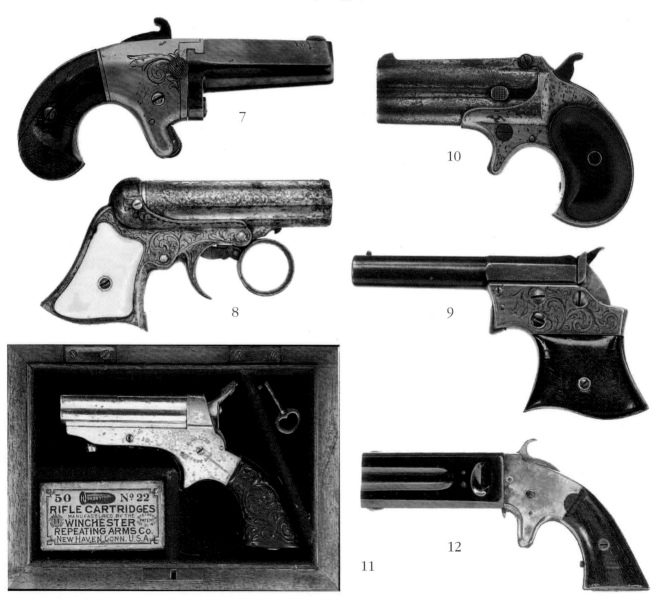

7

10

8

9

11

12

2
Towns of the Old West

The look and feel of old Western towns is so completely familiar. We can easily imagine walking down the dusty boardwalk, pushing through a pair of swing doors into the saloon. The classic frontier town looks flimsy, just like an ephemeral movie set, and the insubstantial, flat-fronted buildings have a wonderful cinematic quality. They usually started as one-street towns, with hitching rails in front of the buildings. This thoroughfare would be lined with archetypal Western institutions: saloons, trading posts, sheriffs' offices, livery stables, banks, gunsmiths, and telegraph offices. As they became more

Opposite page: *Offices for the mail company, the telegraph office, and stores supplying dry goods, groceries, and liquor–a recurring theme in the Western town.*

Left: *The grand sounding St. James' Saloon in Dodge City is typical of bars of the period.*

established, a Wells Fargo Office, a Texas Rangers' office, newspaper office, barbershop, town jail, apothecary, dentist, photographer, or hotel might also have opened for business. Many towns also catered for the more spiritual side of life by establishing a church, and every town of the Old West required its own cemetery. Western towns reflected the preoccupations of the West itself: cattle, gold, the law, fighting, gambling, and good times.

Throughout John Wayne's Western career, the archetypal Western town appears as a "character" in many of his movies. Perhaps one of the most poignant of these locations is the real life town of Carson City, Nevada; the backdrop to Wayne's final film, *The Shootist*. When legendary gunfighter J. B. Books is diagnosed with cancer, he refuses to leave the town at the behest of the Marshal, and insists that he will stay there to die.

Just as Carson City grew up as a trading post on the California Trail, thousands of Western towns sprang up as frontier life developed. They grew up at railheads, along cattle trails, near gold fields and silver mines, and around military forts. They were often isolated and surrounded by miles of empty, threatening wilderness. Western civilization was completely different than that of the East. The landscape was bigger, and the towns were smaller.

Above: *The blacksmith often set up shop in a field before a permanent forge could be built. This one is at Guthrie, Oklahoma, around 1889.*

Opposite page: *The stage comes to town! As this re-enactment shows, the arrival of the stage was an eagerly anticipated event in most Western towns, bringing mail and goods from back East.*

Overleaf: *A Western town in the making; temporary bank buildings and the beginnings of a lodging house in Perry, Oklahoma.*

Left: *The Boomers camp at Arkansas City, Kansas, in 1893. The tent's occupants were waiting for the land rush to start. Guthrie, which was to become Oklahoma's first state capital, went from a tent town like this to one having three newspapers, a hotel, three general stores, and fifty saloons in five months.*

Below: *Wild Bill Hickok was brought in as Town Marshal in Abilene to try to introduce some form of law and order. This was a challenge faced by many growing Western towns.*

Abilene was the first true "cow town" in the United States; J. C. McCoy established the cattle market there in 1867, and the business soon escalated. 600,000 heads of cattle were driven into the town in a single year, and the cows were then railroaded on the hoof to cities in the East. By 1871 Abilene was a boom town, wild, woolly, and loud, full of dusty cowboys and cattle drivers. As the town spiralled out of control, the authorities brought in Wild Bill Hickok as Marshal. Although he successfully introduced gun control, he failed to establish the kind of peace the townsfolk longed for. Ultimately, Abilene decided to forgo the income from the cattle drives, and the business went to other stops on the line, such as Ellsworth, Newton, and Dodge City itself, the last and most wicked of the Kansas cattle towns.

The early establishment of law and order was crucial to the development of these towns from shiftless camps into permanent settlements. Where this proved impossible, towns were often abandoned. Towns whose water or gold ran out and towns bypassed by the railroads or cattle trails shared this ignominious fate. Life

Left: *Abilene, Kansas, in 1879. The false fronted wooden buildings furthest down the street are beginning to be replaced by more grand brick built ones like the edifice with splendid eagle atop on the right of the picture.*

Left: *Abilene in 1882. By then it had elevated itself from a wild cattle town to a relatively peaceful residence of farmers, merchants, and ordinary citizens.*

Above: *Ellsworth in 1872.
J. Mueller's Shop catered for
the footwear needs of the
locals against a background
of cowtown wildness.*

Left: *The main street in
Dodge City warning against
carrying arms in the town.
These laws were strictly
enforced by The Dodge City
Peace Commission.*

Left: *The Dodge City Peace Commission as it was composed in 1883. Back (left to right): W. H. Harris, Luke Short, Bat Masterson, W. F. Petillon (added later), Front: C. E. Bassett, Wyatt Earp, L. Mclean, Neil Brown.*

in the Old West was extremely volatile, and new arrivals searched about restlessly, looking for land and opportunity. Many new towns were founded and abandoned a few years later.

The saloon was often the first building in a Western town and might start out as just a tent or lean-to. When it became more permanent, it might also be used as a public meeting-house. Brown's Hole near the Wyoming-Colorado-Utah border was the first drinking house to become known as a saloon, back in 1822, and catered to the regions fur trappers. A town often had more than one saloon, often completely disproportionate to its population. Livingstone, Montana, for example had a population of only 3,000 but no fewer than 33 saloons. Saloons often served liquor (whiskey, bourbon, rye, and beer) twenty-four hours a day, and their clientele reflected a cross-section of the West's white male population. These men included cowboys, gunmen, lawmen, and gamblers. Women, Chinese, and black Americans were unwelcome, while it was

Above and overleaf: *Many towns that sprang up in the middle of nowhere to service the cattle or mining industries failed, died, and were abandoned a few years later becoming "ghost" towns.*

Far left: *Wichita, Kansas, in 1871 still in its cowtown infancy with liquor and cigar stores in evidence alongside a wooden hotel.*

Left: *Local patrons gather round outside Kelley's saloon, The Bijou, at Round Pond, Oklahoma, in 1894. The saloon became an important social center in frontier times.*

Below: *Bader & Laubner's saloon in Dodge City during the 1880s.*

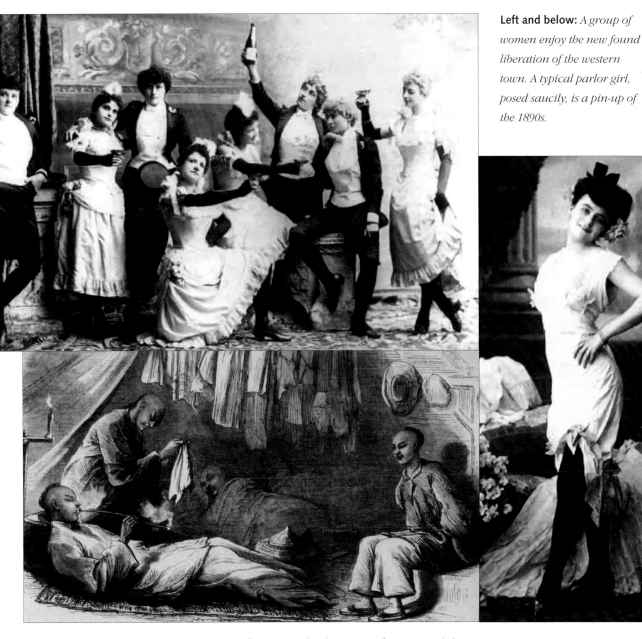

Left and below: *A group of women enjoy the new found liberation of the western town. A typical parlor girl, posed saucily, is a pin-up of the 1890s.*

Above left: *Much of the hard work in building the railroad network that put many new towns on the map was done by Chinese immigrants who lived in very basic conditions.*

actually illegal for Indians to enter. Of course, the barring of women did not extend to the saloon girls who worked in the establishments, selling over-priced drinks to the customers, and keeping them company. Surprisingly, very few of these women were prostitutes. But many saloon proprietors were criminals and gunmen, in same way that many wayward women ran bordellos. These included Wyatt Earp, Bob Ford (Jesse James's killer), Doc Holliday, Luke Short, and Wild Bill Hickok.

As the West became more sophisticated, saloons offered a variety of entertainment including fine dining, billiards, singing, dancing, and bowling. But the primary saloon pastimes were drinking and gambling. Almost every saloon had a poker table and spittoons, and many different card games were played. Of course, gaming often led to violence, which regularly spilled out onto the street. A complex "bar etiquette" also prevailed, which governed the buying and accepting of drinks. Breeches of this unwritten code could also lead to serious trouble. John Wayne himself was known for his love of alcohol, and his biographer Michael Munn maintained that a morning filming schedule was necessary due to the fact that by most afternoons, he "was a mean drunk."

Equally important to every town was its general store, or trading post. Without it, it would be almost impossible for a town to get off the ground. It has often been remarked that some of the biggest fortunes made in the Old West were made, not by miners or settlers, but by the tradesmen who supplied them. Depending on their location, the general store would stock farm supplies, mining equipment, or cowboy gear. They also carried basic foodstuffs and seeds to get the "sodbuster" farmers started, while they removed the prairie turf to plant their crops. The general store would also supply the townsfolk with their basic needs. Perhaps the most famous Western store in popular culture is the Oleson's general store in Laura Ingalls Wilder's hometown of Walnut Grove, Minnesota. The Oleson's ambiguous social status is also interesting. While storekeepers were vital to the development of the West, many used their virtual monopolies to charge extortionate prices. General stores and trading posts were also great social centers, where news and gossip were exchanged. In *True Grit* (1969) Wayne's character (U. S. Marshal Rooster Cogburn) lodges in the back of a Chinese dry-goods store in Fort Smith, Arkansas.

After a few years of manic prosperity, many Western towns simply disappeared from the map. The region is scattered with ghostly, abandoned towns, many of whose eerie streets have not heard a footstep, or a hoof beat, for years.

As the original settlers moved further and further west into Indian Territory, they constructed military outposts as a first step to some kind of security. The origins of the majority of frontier forts date back to the early part

Right: *The interior of a recreated Western store. This was a vital factor in the sustainability of most towns supplying everything from food to ammunition, brooms to fancy clothes.*

of the nineteenth century. Most were in use for the greater part of that century, changing their function as the turbulent history of those decades rolled out. Many forts also formed the nucleus of frontier settlements that became the major towns and cities of today. Wayne himself expressed his views on this wave of Western expansion in a 1971 interview with *Playboy*: "I don't feel we did wrong in taking this great country away from them [the Indians]... our so-called stealing of this country was just a question of survival. There were great numbers of people who needed new land the Indians were selfishly trying to keep it for themselves... you can't whine and bellyache 'cause somebody else got a break and you didn't, like these Indians are."

In many ways, the history and development of Fort Smith in Arkansas is fairly typical of the frontier fort, and became critical in the enforcement of frontier justice. The town is also the backdrop to one of Wayne's most influential roles, that of U. S. Marshal Reuben "Rooster" J. Cogburn in *True Grit* (1969). In Wayne's only Oscar-winning performance, he portrays a Civil War veteran, who

Above: *Indians in an idyllic setting before the onrush of white settlers into the West. Their way of life was effectively destroyed in the span of 100 years.*

lost his eye fighting for the Confederate guerrilla leader, William Quantrill. In *True Grit*, Cogburn is a U. S. Marshal, one of the many appointed by the famous "Hanging" Judge Isaac Parker to keep the peace in the roughest parts of the Indian Territory. Ironically, in the man-hunting quest at the heart of the drama, Cogburn is partnered by another Western icon, a Texas Ranger (LaBoeuf). The first ten rangers had been assembled by Stephen F. Austin in 1823 to protect the small number of families settling in the state.

Judge Parker himself disembarked in Fort Smith from the steamship *Ella Hughes* on May 4, 1875, and remained in the town until his death. President Grant had appointed him to the position of Federal District Judge for Western Arkansas. Even by Territory standards, Fort Smith was desperately in need of law-bringers. The town was a focus of lawlessness, its streets often walked by the likes of the Daltons, Bill Powers, Dick Broadwell, Henry Starr, and Jim Reed.

Historically, Fort Smith had been the first Frontier fort constructed in Arkansas. It was originally built in 1817, at the junction of the Poteau and Arkansas rivers, at the southern edge of the Ozarks. The role of its garrison was to patrol Indian Territory and to promote peace between the indigenous Osage and the incoming Cherokee, and troops based at Fort Smith attempted to keep hunting disputes from flaring into outright war between the two tribes. John

Below: *An early photograph Judge Isaac Parker aged 35.*

Left: *The confluence of the Poteau and Arkansas rivers, where the original fort was built.*

Rogers founded the town around the fort in the 1820s. His smart brick house, built in the early 1840s, still stands at 400 North Eighth Street.

The first military fort on the site was abandoned in 1824, but the town of Fort Smith became an important staging post on the notorious "Trail of Tears." This was the route ordained for the forced removal of five native tribes (the Cherokees, Choctaws, Chickasaws, Creeks, and Seminoles) under the terms of the 1830 Indian Removal Act. This act decreed that these dispossessed tribes should be removed to the lands west of the Mississippi. Between 1830 and 1850, 100,000 Indians undertook the journey along the infamous Trail, and many perished. For the remainder of the century, Fort Smith reflected both the history of the nation and the U.S. government's turbulent Indian policy.

A second Fort Smith was begun in 1838 on a 306-acre plot bought for $15,000. It was completed in 1846 at a cost of $300,000. It became the "Motherpost of the Southwest," supplying military forts throughout the Southwest. In 1858, Fort Smith became a stop on the overland mail route that connected the East to the West.

Fort Smith began the Civil War on the Confederate side, with two companies of the Confederate cavalry garrisoned at the military post, commanded by Captain Samuel Sturgis. But at the outbreak of war, Sturgis abandoned the position almost immediately, though Rebel cavalry units from Texas, Louisiana, and Arkansas soon reoccupied it. But when Federal troops reasserted their control of Indian Territory in 1863, Fort Smith came under intense pressure and ultimately fell to the Union on September 2, 1863. The Federal occupiers immediately reinforced Fort Smith's defences with rifle pits, trenches, and artillery emplacements. The town came under renewed attack from Rebel troops, but these forces had given up the siege less than a month later. For the rest of the war, Fort Smith provided refuge to many, including former slaves fleeing the South, and frontier families dispossessed by the war. This generosity put pressure on the town's food supply, and in February 1865, the townsfolk were forced to ask President Lincoln for emergency food and supplies.

In the post-war years, the troops at Fort Smith became active participants in the Reconstruction of the South, controlling U.S. troops in Arkansas, Texas, and Indian Territory. In 1871, the military post at Fort Smith was abandoned for a second time, and the Infantry troops finally withdrew in September that year.

Below: *The officer's quarters at the old fort became Fort Smith's courtroom and the basement became the jail.*

In Fort Smith's post-military period, the settlement became an increasingly pivotal frontier town. In 1872, the federal district court for the Western District of Arkansas was relocated from Van Buren, Arkansas, to Fort Smith's refurbished officers' barracks. It was this transfer that led to Parker's appointment in the town. When the judge arrived in 1875, the *Fort Smith Herald* remarked, "We have met the Judge and were favorably impressed with his appearance—open and manly in expression, and apparently a sociable and affable gentlemen." Parker and his family took up residence in the stone commissary building of the old fort. At this time, Fort Smith had no paved streets, sidewalks, streetlights, factories, good hotels, or schools. The judge described Indian Territory in his correspondence, saying, "the facilities for transport are meager and primitive. The country is sparsely settled." It was also a focus of criminality. The end of the Civil War had unleashed a tide of racial violence and unchecked lawlessness. Many criminals moved west to Indian Territory, trying to outrun the law. They roamed the wild country, raping, murdering, and looting, with very little intervention from the authorities.

The installation of Parker as the area's lone Federal Judge was designed to counterbalance this desperate state of anarchy. He went on to appoint two hundred United States Marshals to police an area of 74,000 square miles, sparsely inhabited by 60,000 people. Sixty-five of these men eventually would

Right: Taken at Vinita, Oklahoma, this group of U.S. Marshals was involved in a fight with outlaw Ned Christie in November 1892.

Left: A group of U.S. Marshals, which is part of a panoramic photograph of a reunion around 1900.

Left and right: *George Maledon, Fort Smith's eccentric hangman. He hung 60 lawbreakers and shot 2 more when they tried to escape. Right: Maledon often appeared fully armed at his hangings.*

Below: *The hanging of Cherokee Bill aka Crawford Goldsby on March 17, 1896.*

lose their lives trying to impose the rule of law. John Wayne's iconic Marshal was one of these stalwart individuals, and his character had a second outing in the 1975 film, *Rooster Cogburn*. Although Parker was salaried at $2,000 a year, Marshals like Cogburn were only paid bounties and rewards.

It took Parker no time at all to earn his "Hanging" soubriquet. On September 3, 1875, six convicted men swung from the newly constructed Fort Smith gallows. During the Judge's tenure at the Fort Smith courthouse, he tried 13,490 cases, 344 of which were for capital offences. Parker secured 9,454 convictions, and sentenced 160 men and women to hang. Seventy-nine of these sentences were implemented. Parker's famous henchman, George Maledon ("the Prince of Hangmen"), despatched sixty of these condemned criminals, and shot two more as they tried to escape justice. Parker's courtroom became the most famous in the West. It was the scene of more judicial execution than any other place in American history.

As well as hanging the lawless, Parker also imprisoned many criminals under the Fort Smith courthouse. During her 1885 trip to Indian Territory, Anna Davies (the daughter of Senator Henry Davies), christened his infamous jail "Hell on the Border."

Parker's court retained a great deal of autonomous power until September 1896, when it was finally stripped of its authority over Indian Territory. This followed a national trend towards centralized, federal authority, but seems to have been precipitated by Cherokee Bill's notorious escape from the Fort Smith jailhouse in the summer of 1895, during which a prison guard was killed.

Left: *The interior of Judge Parker's courtroom in session.*

Below: *Judge Parker's courtroom is preserved at the Fort Smith National Historic Site.*

Parker died just two months later, worn out from years of overwork. Despite his violent reputation, his obituary described him as "one of God's noblemen... [with] a great heart."

Fort Smith had several other famous residents, including Frank Dalton, the (surprisingly) law-abiding brother of the Dalton Gang members. He was appointed Fort Smith's Deputy Marshal in 1884, and was shot dead trying to arrest Dave Smith, a local horse thief. The infamous Pearl Starr was also a local

Above: *Judge Parker's gallows remain at Fort Smith, clearly recognizable from the illustration on the previous page.*

Right: *What remains of the original officer's quarters and the old jail are preserved at Fort Smith as a National Historic Site. The old Napoleon cannon is a relic of the Civil War.*

brothel and saloon keeper. Pearl was the daughter of the notorious female bandit, Belle Starr, and had become a prostitute after her mother's early demise in a shootout. A sharp businesswoman, she soon graduated to keeping her own bordello, signed with a bright red star surrounded by lighted "pearls." Pearl boasted that her establishment had the most beautiful girls west of the

Far right: *More residents of lawless Fort Smith; outlaw Belle Starr with her Indian husband, Blue Duck.*

Above: *Pearl Starr, the daughter of outlaw Belle Starr, ran a notorious brothel in Fort Smith.*

Left: *A studio portrait of Judge Isaac Parker in his prime.*

Right: *The ignominious end of the Dalton gang at Coffeyville, Kansas, in 1892. With the growing civilisation of the Frontier towns, thanks to the likes of Judge Parker, by this time outlaws like them were running out of places to be bad in.*

Mississippi, piano music, and good liquor. The brothel was extremely successful, and Starr invested in several other Fort Smith businesses. She was finally run out of town in 1921, when the town authorities finally made prostitution illegal.

As well as *True Grit*, Fort Smith has also provided the setting and inspiration behind several other famous Western movies and television films. These included *Hang 'Em High* (1968) starring Clint Eastwood; *Frank and Jesse* (1994) starring Bill Paxton and Rob Lowe; the Civil War mini-series *The Blue and the Gray* (1982); and *Lonesome Dove* (1989). The original location of the town's two military forts was designated a National Historic Site in 1960. In honor of its great contribution to enforcing law and order on the West, the town is now the location of the United States Marshal's Service National Museum.

TIM EVANS   BOB DALTON   GROT DALTON   DICK BROADWE

BANK ROBBERY COFFEYVILLE KANS

3
The Big Trail West

The American mindset was transformed forever by the Louisiana Purchase of 1803. President Thomas Jefferson paid $15 million to Emperor Napoleon of France for 800,000 square miles of territory, located between the Mississippi and the Rockies. Jefferson was a great intellect, and fascinated by everything from dinosaurs to fine wine, but had been spellbound by tales of the West from his boyhood. By the time of the "Purchase," he had amassed the largest collection of books about the West on earth. Jefferson then persuaded Congress to authorize $2,500 to finance the westward expedition of adventurers Meriwether Lewis and William Clark. Lewis was Jefferson's personal secretary, a skilled hunter and amateur scientist, while Clark was Jefferson's old army commander and a talented woodsman. The main purpose of the Lewis-Clark expedition was to explore the newly acquired territory. Jefferson's other objective was to locate the (non-existent) Northwest Passage. Instead, Lewis and Clark were to become the first white Americans to cross the Rockies, and by doing this, they thus established an overland route to the West. Their courage and tenacity blazed a trail for other adventurers, such as Kit Carson, Jim Bridger, Bill Williams, and Joe Walker.

The way West was now open to the early frontiers people, and as the great Western writer Louis L'Amour wrote, "There was no period in the world's history that is so fascinating as the era in which the American West was opening up."

The way West was a huge influence on John Wayne's early life. His own family had made their way out West, travelling from Winterset, Iowa, to Southern California for the sake of Wayne's father's health. The family became homesteaders on an 80-acre farm.

The motives of the early settlers were variable, but, as one commentator

Above: *John Wayne won his first starring role in* The Big Trail *of 1930.*

Left: *Two covered wagons dwarfed by the monumental Western scenery.*

claimed, "They agreed in one general object–that of bettering their condition." Early visitors to the west coast commented on the healthy climate, and rumors spread about the fertile land there. Potential emigrants were told that "the wheat grew as tall as a man, with each stalk sprouting seven kernels," and turnips were "five feet tall."

From the Mid-West, the overland journey West was around two thousand miles, and took around six months. As well as requiring bravery and enterprise, the trip was also expensive. It cost around a thousand dollars for a family to join a wagon train and fit themselves out. The price tag for a specially prepared "covered" wagon was around four hundred dollars. This would be equipped with a canvas top, waterproofed with linseed oil, and stretched over a framework of steel "hoops." Wagons usually had wooden wheels, and were not equipped with brakes or springs. They were usually pulled by oxen, which were strong and easy to work, and could be used as a farm animal when the settlers reached their destination. The settlers sometimes used horses and mules to pull the wagons, but these were more difficult to handle, and more likely to be stolen by Indians. At the start of the journey, the settlers loaded the wagons with provisions and

Above: *Kit Carson helped open the trails to the West.*

Left: *A typical pioneer wagon. These enabled women to accompany their men folk on the journey West.*

tools. They could carry as much as 2,500 pounds in weight, but 1,600 pounds was more usual. This would be made up from food, cooking utensils, water, farm tools, and a shovel. A typical family packed 800 pounds of flour, 700 pounds of bacon, 200 pounds of lard, 200 pounds of beans, 100 pounds of fruit, 75 pounds of coffee, and 25 pounds of salt. Sometimes families packed their furniture, but this was often abandoned en route.

The mental picture we have of the settlers riding the wagon is actually quite misleading. There was little room in the wagon for people and so only small children and the elderly rode. Everyone else walked alongside the slowly

Below: *Oxen were most often used to draw the loaded wagons West.*

Above: *An idyllic representation of the wagon train.*

rolling wagons. This meant that the wagon train travelled at around two miles an hour, or an average of ten miles a day.

The epic story of Westward expansion and the story of the wagon trains also became pivotal to Wayne's movie career. Aged just 23, Wayne was cast in his first starring role in *The Big Trail* (1930), that of young adventurer Breck Coleman. Suspecting Red Flack (Tyrone Power Sr.) of the murder of an old friend, Coleman joins a wagon train of settlers making their way West under Flack's supervision. Raoul Walsh's film was pioneering in its use of the panoramic western scenery, and his attention to detail in making the wagon train itself as authentic as possible. Just like the wagons of the early settlers, Walsh's were pulled by oxen. His characters wore grimy and dust-stained clothes, and even the food supplies the immigrants carried with them were researched to make the "trek" look and feel as real as possible. Locations in five states were used to represent the settlers' journey West.

Much later in his career, John Wayne was to be part of one of the most epic film portraits of Westward expansion ever made, *How the West was Won* (1962). The movie consists of five segments, that follow four generations of the Prescott family as they journey from New York state to the Pacific Ocean. Westward migration is the fundamental theme of the film. It was inspired by a much longer and more complex series of historical narratives that appeared as a photo essay series in *Life Magazine*. Louis L'Amour then wrote the "book of the film." The movie evokes the feeling that an entire continent is responding to some magnetic westward impulse. Hawkins, Louis L'Amour's river pirate character, graphically describes the trek west as a "colossal binge, a gigantic migration... The world had never seen the like, folks from all the land of creation, streamin' west, flowin' like a great tide, some of them walkin', some

Below: *The wagons struggled to cross the Rockies.*

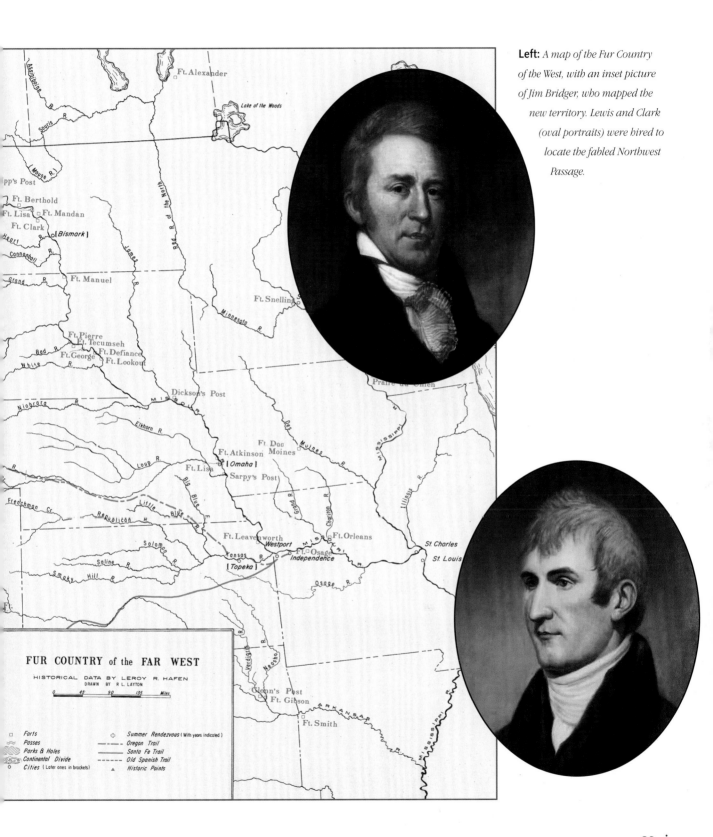

FUR COUNTRY of the FAR WEST

HISTORICAL DATA BY LEROY R. HAFEN
DRAWN BY R L LAYTON

0   45   90   135   Miles

☐ Forts	✛ Summer Rendezvous (With years indicated)
Passes	Oregon Trail
Parks & Holes	Santa Fe Trail
Continental Divide	Old Spanish Trail
○ Cities (Later ones in brackets)	▲ Historic Points

drivin' wagons, and some a-horseback... to populate a new land." "West was the magic word. It was the 'Open Sesame' to fantastic futures."

How the West was Won is made up from five distinct segments, set between 1839 and 1889: "The Rivers," "The Plains," "The Civil War," "The Railroad," and "The Outlaws." The final section is staged in the San Francisco of the 1880s. John Wayne plays General Tecumseh Sherman in the civil war piece, which was directed by his old friend John Ford. The huge project was studded with a plethora of movie luminaries, including Henry Fonda, Gregory Peck, George Peppard, Debbie Reynolds, James Stewart, and Spencer Tracey.

As the wagons rolled West, pioneer groups often fell into two categories, "stickers," and "movers." "Stickers" moved West in stages, sometimes over several generations (like the Prescotts), or settled permanently along the route.

Below: *Many pioneers died en route to the West, and were buried where they fell.*

"Movers" kept going until they reached the Frontier. Many people died en route, their pathetic graves marked only with wooden crosses.

Settlers that finally made it to the West needed a great deal of courage and resilience to tame this strange and lonely land. Mental readjustment was also required to the western landscape. What the first people arriving in the West ultimately found was somewhat reminiscent of the East in the sixteenth century. Fluid communities sprang up, and died down just as quickly when overtaken by misfortune: disease, Indian attack, or natural disaster. Not only were the pure in heart lured West by opportunity. Gamblers, cardsharps, land-grabbers, villains, and prostitutes also followed the trail West. Law-abiding settlers had to avoid any number of dangers and pitfalls, both man-made and natural. But just like the ocean voyages of the first white Americans, journeying West remained a metaphor for freedom and personal fulfilment. This is almost certainly why John Wayne was so attracted to making Western movies; it gave him the chance to get

Above: *A wagon train reaches journey's end on the West coast.*

4
Cattle Drives and Cowboys

Oh, he would twirl that lariat and he didn't do it slow

He could catch them forefeet nine out of ten for any kind of dough

And when the herd stamped he was always on the spot

And set them to milling, like the stirrings of a pot

The Cowboy

Of all the West's iconic characters, perhaps the cowboy is the most universally recognized and admired. This certainly became true for John Wayne. Almost all of the most defining roles in his career were in Westerns, and many featured cowboys and ranchers. His first starring role was in the 1930 movie *The Big Trail*. It was a big budget spectacular filmed in "grandeur" to take advantage of the wide and magnificent Western scenery. Several of his Western roles were pivotal to his career, and constructed the image he presented to the American public of the morally strong, tough man of few words: Cord McNally in *Rio Lobo* (1970), John Bernard Books in *The Shootist* (1976).

Ironically, the cowboy role that has come to symbolize the free spirit of America originated in Spain. The Conquistadors brought their cow-handling skills to South America in the sixteenth century; the *vaqueros* had learned how to herd large numbers of horses and cattle across the open lands to forage. These original "cowpunchers" were usually mounted on horseback, but also used donkeys, or burros. "Cowboy," the English-language equivalent of the Spanish term, made its first appearance between 1715 and 1725. By this time, the cattle industry was becoming an increasingly important element of the North American economy, particularly in the South and West. "Boy" was by no means meant to demean. Tough work like this required youth and vigor, and real boys as young as twelve were

Below: *A poster for John Wayne's 1935 movie,* The New Frontier.

employed in ranch work. As European settlers brought Longhorn cattle to the New World, a culture of ranching became established, particularly in the South. Ironically, the market for beef was very limited at this time, and the animals were mainly bred for their hides and tallow. The state of Texas (independent from 1836), soon became prominent in the American cattle trade. Anglo-Texans drove out many Mexican ranchers and confiscated their animals. This new breed of

cattlemen soon developed its own cowboy-ing traditions. Typically the Texas cowboy was a solitary drifter, who worked for a different outfit every season. By contrast, the Californian "cowboy tradition" was for men to live together on permanent ranches. More verdant grazing meant that there was less open range, and Californian meat tended to stay in the region, which meant far fewer cattle drives. The Californian ranching system dated back many years. There were already nineteen *rancheros* by 1790, and this number was greatly increased by 1836. Spanish mission farmlands were seized by the Mexican government, and redistributed, often in huge tracts, to favored ranchers as grazing land.

California's ranch-based cowboys (also known as "buckaroos") had a much more settled, domestic existence than their Texan counterparts, and were considered more skilled in animal husbandry. Because their lifestyles were more predictable, and less dangerous, many of these men married, settled on their home ranches, and raised families.

Top right: *A posed photograph of a roped steer, taken in Graham County, Arizona, in the 1890s.*

Left: *A romantic view of a cowboy camp at night.*

Bottom right: *Mounted cowboys with a roped steer.*

A third class of cowhand, the Florida cowhunter, or "cracker cowboy," had a completely different modus operandi. Spanish settlers had introduced cattle to the state in the sixteenth century, and the cowhunters themselves were usually of Spanish or Indian origin. These men used dogs and bullwhips, rather than Western lassos, to control the smaller breeds of cattle native to this region. Historically, meat produced in Florida was used to supply the Spanish missions in the north of the state, and the island of Cuba, but became of critical importance to the Confederacy during the Civil War. It was so important that in March of 1864, the 800-strong "Cow Cavalry" (the 1st Battalion Florida Special Cavalry) was formed to protect the cattle from Union raiders.

The cowboy tradition also developed outside the United States. The Canadian cattle industry was focused on Alberta and Saskatchewan, and many of its cowboys were American. Elsewhere, Hawaii had its paniolos; Argentina its gauchos; Peru its chalans; Chile its huasos; Mexico its vaqueros and charros; and Australia its stockmen and drovers. Each of these regions had wide-open spaces for grazing cattle, sheep, or horses, and developed their own herding techniques and traditions.

Wherever cowboys worked, the life was almost always hard, potentially dangerous, and lonely. The pay was meager, and the profession carried a lowly social status. Their melancholy permeated the rich cowhand culture of songs and poems.

The defeat of the Southern states in the Civil War had a great effect on the cattle industry, leading to a kind of cowboy diaspora. When Texans went off to fight in the war, their cattle were left to roam free, and huge herds built up. There was now no market for the five million cattle stranded in the economically crippled South, while the industrial North was desperate for meat. To drive the cattle north was extremely difficult, time-consuming, and dangerous, and this meant that cowboy skills were in high demand. The Civil War also had had an impact on the racial mix of the men following the profession. Many freed slaves were attracted to the freedom of riding the range, and as many as 5,000, or one-quarter, of the men riding the line in Texas were African-Americans. Mexicans also became cowboys, as did men from several Indian tribes including the Creeks, Seminoles, and Timucuas. Once the war was over, many Civil War veterans returned to life on the range.

Originally, the Texan herds were driven across Missouri on their way to the north and east, but the cattlemen ran into increasing hostility from the local farmers, who objected to the damage that the cattle drives caused. Many also believed that the cows carried a virulent tick that was deadly to their livestock.

In effect, this standoff meant that thousands of cattle were marooned in

Above: *A Paiute Indian shows his skill in roping; many Indians became successful cowboys.*

Texas, where they were worth only $4 a head, prevented from moving to the more industrialized parts of the nation, where they could be sold for in excess of $40 a head. This economic opportunity was not lost on entrepreneurial cattlemen like Joseph G. McCoy, who persuaded the Kansas Pacific Railroad to build a siding at Abilene, Kansas. He then constructed a huge complex of stockyards, where cattle could be held before being loaded onto the eastbound railroad. He then encouraged the Texan ranchers to bring their stock to Abilene.

In 1867, he was responsible for shipping 35,000 head of cattle, but this was

Above: *Caldwell, Kansas, was a major cowtown. This photograph from the early 1880s shows the Southwestern Hotel.*

to increase exponentially to 600,000 head in 1871. One of the main routes used by the herders to get to McCoy's Abilene stockyards was the Chisholm Cattle Trail. This dirt track route was named for Jesse Chisholm. Chisholm had built several trading posts, before the outbreak of the Civil War, alongside what was to become the Oklahoma section of the Trail. Sadly, Jesse Chisholm died in 1868, and never drove cattle along the route that bore his name. The first cattleman to use the Trail, to drive Texan cattle from San Antonio to the railhead at Abilene, was O. W. Wheeler. In 1867, Wheeler succeeded in herding 2,400 steers along the route to Abilene. Ultimately, Chisholm's dirt track was to be trodden by upwards of five million cattle, and a million mustangs. It became an important financial artery, and aided the recovery of the South from the devastation of the Civil War. Based on the Jr. Borden Chase story *The Chisholm Trail,* the 1948 film *Red River* follows the dramatic action as Wayne's character, rancher Thomas Dunson, drives his herd to Abilene. Abilene was the first true "cow town" in the

U.S.; Illinois businessman J. G. McCoy established the cattle market there in 1867. Over 600,000 head of cattle were driven into the town in a single year, and were then railroaded on the hoof to the Eastern cities. According to the Western writer Louis L'Amour, "Abilene in 1871 was a booming town, but the boom was almost over... [it was] wild and woolly, and it was loud," full of dusty cowboys and drivers. Abilene's town authorities brought in Wild Bill Hickok as Marshal to try and tame the town. But although Hickok introduced gun control, he failed to establish the kind of peace the townsfolk longed for. They decided to forgo the income from the cattle drives, and the business went to other stops on the line, such as Ellsworth, Newton, and Dodge City.

In its original form, the Chisholm Trail began in San Antonio, and ended at Abilene. But it gradually extended further into Kansas, first to Newton, then to Wichita, and finally to Caldwell (by 1883). The long drive from Texas to Kansas took between two and three months, and was enough to challenge even the most experienced Texas cattlemen. The cattle moved along at around ten to twelve miles a day, which allowed them to graze as they went. The terrain itself was extremely difficult. The herdsmen had to drive the cattle across two major rivers (the Arkansas and the Red), together with various creeks, canyons, mountains, and badlands along the route. But ruthless cattle rustlers and predatory Indians were enough to challenge even the most fearless cattlemen. (Oklahoma was still Indian Territory at this time.) There was also the ever-present danger of stampede from the capricious Texan Longhorn.

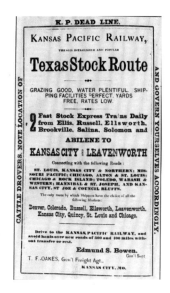

Below: *The main street at Ellsworth in 1872.*

The mastering of these diverse problems greatly enhanced the reputation of the Texas cowboy, and he achieved an almost folkloric status. Specialist trailing contractors managed most of these drives, and they recruited bands of cowboys to ride the line. Over the years, these trail bosses perfected an economic system of cattle driving that meant they could get the animals to market for around sixty to seventy-five cents a head. This was far cheaper than sending the cattle by rail. These highly skilled professional drovers included rugged individuals like John T. Lyle, George W. Slaughter, and the Pryor brothers.

The Great Western Cattle Trail ran roughly parallel to the Chisholm Trail, to the West. It ran from Bandera, Texas, to Dodge City, Kansas. Doan's Crossing was the last supply post on the Trail before the lands of the Indian Nation. C. E. Doan was the proprietor of the trading post there, and kept a tally of the beasts moving through. The peak of the traffic occurred in 1881, when 301,000 head of cattle passed through. The largest individual herd to go through consisted of 10,000 animals. But the Trail became increasingly dangerous as the Cheyenne and Arapaho tribes were confined to reservations. Now that the wild antelope and buffalo were nearly extinct, being restricted to these "meatless" lands effectively meant a lingering starvation for the natives. They tried to survive by demanding a "trail bounty" of beef from each passing herd. If the trail bosses refused to pay, the Indians retaliated by attacking the drive, or making the cattle stampede.

Above and left: *A classic round-up scene at the Sherman Ranch in Kansas. The Texas Longhorn was well suited to the arid conditions of the Southwest.*

Perhaps the most famous trail route of all was the Goodnight-Loving Trail. Charles Goodnight and Oliver Loving formed a partnership when they met in 1867, and started a cattle drive from Young County in Texas to Fort Summer in New Mexico. The greatest real-life cowboy of them all, Charles Goodnight was born in Illinois in 1836, but his family trekked West in 1846, the so-called Year of Decision. In New Mexico 8,000 Navajo tribes-people were confined. Virtually starving for the want of meat, these Indians were the responsibility of government agents who were desperately trying to procure meat for them. To avoid the threat of Indian attack, the partners decided to drive their herd around the Texas Panhandle, which was teeming with warlike Comanches. This involved taking a much longer and completely arid route through the "most desolate country." Three hundred cattle died in the heat and a hundred more thirst-crazed beasts drowned in a stampede at the Pecos River. Goodnight sold half of the surviving herd to the reservation agents, and then continued the drive into Colorado, selling the remaining animals in Denver. The whole escapade netted the huge sum of $24,000, and the reputation for forging the most famous trail route of all time. Sadly, Oliver Loving was to be shot by a Comanche brave, and die of septicaemia. Goodnight described him as "one of the coolest and bravest men I have ever known, but devoid of caution."

The Goodnight-Loving Trail originally ran southwest to the Horsehead Crossing on the Pecos River to Fort Sumner. In 1871, Goodnight extended the route to join up with the Fort Worth and Denver City Railroad at Grenada, Colorado, where many cattle were sold to gold diggers. Ultimately, the Trail went as far as Cheyenne, Wyoming. Charles Goodnight had a huge influence on the culture of the West, and is even credited with having coined the modern use of the term "cowboy." He had a close, almost paternal, relationship with his men, and forbade them to drink, swear, or play cards. This inveterate plainsman was a cattle industry pioneer, and made a huge contribution to the hugely lucrative practice of driving cattle to market.

One of his most important innovations was the invention of the iconic chuck wagon. Drawn by oxen, the wagon was equipped with a chuck box, whose hinged lid dropped down to become a cook's worktable. The truck wagon became an absolutely critical piece of equipment, and was used on the cattle drives for decades. A modern form of this iconic invention remains in use on the larger ranches today.

Above: *John Wayne in the classic* Rio Lobo. *He is dressed in practical Western attire.*

Cattlemen like Goodnight changed the fortunes of the whole region. Having made several fortunes and gone bust several times, he died at his ranch at the age of 93. Rumor has it that he had survived for years on a diet of coffee, beef, and Cuban cigars.

During his Western film career, Wayne played several cattle ranchers and trail bosses. In *The Cowboys* (1972), his character, Montana cattle rancher Wil Andersen, drives his herd to Belle Fourche. While in *The Man Who Shot Liberty Valance* (1962), Wayne plays rancher Tom Doniphon. In *Chisum* (1970), Wayne's character John Chisum demonstrates how even iron-tough cattle barons struggled to protect their ranching way of life from underhanded outsiders.

The heyday of the cattle drives and the trails they used was between 1866 and 1890. Originally, the drives were a major stimulant to the burgeoning railroad network, but as the tracks extended into previously uncharted territory, the need for long and dangerous cattle drives was gradually diminished. They were virtually redundant by the 1890s. The advent of refrigerated cars in the 1880s meant that fresh beef could be transported all the way to Europe by train and ship.

A combination of railroad expansion, the introduction of Joseph E. Glidden's "Devil's Rope" (barbed wire, patented by him in 1874), and irrigation windmills, gradually began to tame the Western plains. It was barbed wire that finally closed down the Chisholm Trail in 1884, and drastically reduced the open routes of most of the Western Trails.

These inventions resulted in a shift away from the open range towards fenced-in ranching, a move which was hastened by the terrible meteorological events of 1886 and 1887. A toxic combination of desperate overgrazing of the prairie (by an estimated 35 to 40 million animals) and atrocious weather conditions led to an ecological disaster. There was an extreme drought in the spring of 1886, followed by a scorching summer, where temperatures on the prairie soared to 109 degrees Fahrenheit. The following January (1887), a tremendous winter storm hit the region, and temperatures fell lower than minus 43 degrees Fahrenheit. A devastating famine ensued, and it is estimated that over half of the prairie cattle succumbed. Many cowboys also perished from cold and hunger. Effectively, the days of the wide-open spaces were numbered, and many cattle operations were bankrupted. The need for private individuals to manage the land properly meant that ranching became much more widespread, and publicly owned grazing land was gradually enclosed. This change in the way the prairie was managed was also helped by the pacification of the Plains tribes. Positively, it went some way to slow down the decimation of the wild buffalo. This more business-like approach also meant that ranches became sound financial investments for cow-savvy entrepreneurs and their financial backers, such as Charles Goodnight and his investor John G. Adair. Huge fortunes were made, and it is estimated that by 1885, just thirty-five cattle barons owned 1.5 million cattle between them. About two-thirds of the Western lands were now being used for grazing.

Not everyone was happy about the cattle ranchers' domination of this entire region. Writing in 1955, Bernard DeVoto wrote a damning description of this system. "The cattlemen came from Elsewhere into the empty West. They were always arrogant and always deluded... They kept sheepmen out of the West... [and] did their utmost to keep the nester, the farmer, the actual settler,

Above: *Charles Goodnight was the greatest Western cowboy of all time.*

the man who could create local and permanent wealth out of the West... the big cattlemen squeezed out the little ones wherever possible... frequently hiring gunmen to murder them."

The move to ranching also led to a changing focus for cowboys, who became more orientated towards animal husbandry than herding. Their new duties included feeding, branding, ear marking, and basic veterinary care. They were also responsible for maintaining the ranch-land, its water supply, and its boundaries.

One of the most recognisable aspects of the classic American cowboy was (and is) his outfit and paraphernalia. His kit evolved over many years, and was driven by practicality. Many of its constituent parts were based on the original

Above: *The interior of a cowboy bunkhouse. Ranch-based cowboys lived in fairly spartan surroundings, but in more comfort than those on the trail.*

1. *Buffalo hide and leather chaps*
2. *Cowboy boots from the 1890s*
3. *Spurs*
4. *One-piece cowboy boots from the 1870s*
5. *Cowboy spurs*
6. *Cowboy spurs*

1. *Mexican sombrero*

2. *Stetson*

3. *Soft felt hat*

4. *Stetson*

outfit of the Mexican vaqueros. Traditionally, the cowboy wore a wide-brimmed hat to protect his face from the sun and snagging branches. It was also high-crowned to keep his head cool. A "stampede string" under the chin kept the hat in place in windy weather and during rough riding. The most famous maker of this kind of headgear was John Batterson Stetson, a professional hatter who popularised a felted version, the "Boss of the Plains," with Western cowboys. The hat was so successful that Stetson built a large national corporation on its popularity. It was worn, and popularized, by a number of Western luminaries, including Buffalo Bill, Annie Oakley, Calamity Jane, and Will Rogers.

Around his neck, the correctly attired cowboy wore a bandanna. This was a large silk or cotton cloth (usually 36 to 44 inches square) that could be used to mop the face, or keep the dust out of his mouth. This neckerchief was also known as a "wild rag" or mascada, and was often elaborately knotted. On his feet, the cowboy wore high-topped boots to protect his lower leg from chafing during long hours in the saddle. The narrow toes helped the cowboy to get his feet into the stirrups, while the high heels kept them there. Many of these boots were also fitted with spurs, to give the rider a stronger leg action. Western spurs are made from metal, and often have a small, serrated wheel attached to them. This was known as the rowel; *la rodaja* or *la estrella* in Spanish. Most cowboys wore sturdy

Below: *A cowboy bandana.*

1. *Studded leather wrist cuffs*
2. *Fringed hide gloves*
3. *Sheepskin-lined coat*
4. *Levi jeans*
5. *Lariat*
6. *Quart*

jeans to prevent tangling with brush or equipment, and were among the first groups of Americans to popularize this practical form of clothing. Levi Strauss opened his eponymous company in San Francisco in 1853, and gained a patent for his famous reinforcing rivet in 1873. The inside leg seams of cowboy jeans were rolled so that they wouldn't rub his legs when he was on horseback. Further protection was offered by leather chaps, or chinks (known in Spanish as *las chaparreras* or *chaparejos*), which were worn over the jeans. These came in many varieties, tailored to the local conditions. Angora chaps, for example, which were covered in long goat hair, were worn for warmth in Wyoming and Montana. Other varieties included batwing chaps, shotgun chaps, woolly chaps, short chaps, and *armistas* chaps. On his hands, the cowboy wore thick hide gloves, to protect his hands from the weather, rope, barbed wire, tools, brush, and vegetation. He might also have a pair of leather wrist cuffs to protect his shirtsleeves. Like the iconic leather jacket worn by many cowboys, these gloves might also be dandified with long leather fringes. For bad weather, the cowboy might also have a slicker or "pommel slicker." This was a long, waterproof coat, designed to protect both the saddle and rider.

The working cowboy collected a modest supply of professional equipment. This might include a quart (a horsewhip made from braided leather), a lariat or lasso (known in Spanish as a *riata* when made from hide, or a *sogo* when made from plant fiber), a leather rope strap, and a bedroll of rolled up blankets. This was also called his dreaming sack.

Although cowboys might have aspired to carry expensive pistols, their weapons were more likely to be ex-Civil War guns, like the Spencer Repeating Rifle. For the slightly better off, the ultimate cowboy weapon was Winchester's 1866 Carbine. This somewhat more sophisticated weapon used rim fire cartridges, and its compact (20 inch) barrel made it easy for a cowboy to stow the gun in his saddle scabbard. With no bolt action, or any other encumbrance, it was swift to draw, fire straight from the saddle, and replace. Larger barrelled guns, such as the Henry Rifle, were also highly regarded on the plains. As well as warding off trouble, cowboys used their weapons to control varmints and shoot game. Heavier rifles, like the Sharps and Spencers, were often used for larger prey, like buffalo.

Knives were also an intrinsic part of every cowboy's equipment, and many carried the famous Bowie knife. Jim Bowie had originated his uniquely curved steel blade in the very early years of the nineteenth century. The knife was designed specifically to be a combined weapon and tool, for use while camping, hunting, and fishing. Bowie himself had used an early version to win his famous Sandbar Fight of 1827. Over the years, he developed many versions of his

Below: *Classic cowboy attire.*

Left and below: *To cowboys on the trail, their most important asset was their horse.*

unique blade. These varied from between six and twelve inches long and one-and-a-half and two inches wide.

But perhaps the most important thing in any cowboy's life was his horse (*caviada* or *caballa* in Spanish), and its tack. Stock horses were bred to make them as effective as possible, and their equipment was developed to suit their tough work. Trail drive horses were bred to be small and light and to have good "cow sense." Essentially, this meant knowing how to control moving cattle. The Morgan, Chickasaw, and Virginia Quarter-Miler were all popular breeds. Some of these are now extinct. Their tack was developed for the comfort and practicality of men who often spent all day in the saddle. The traditional Western saddle has a deep, secure seat with a high pommel and

cantle, and is equipped with wide stirrups. Among other things, the high pommel was also used to store the cowboy's lariat. The comfort of the horse was also considered. The saddle was made with a wide saddletree that distributed the rider's weight over a greater area of the horse's back, and a woollen horse blanket was placed under the saddle to prevent chafing and rubbing. These horse blankets were often woven by Native Americans, or imported from Mexico. At the business end, the Western bridle is usually equipped with a curb bit and has long split reins to give the rider as much control over the horse as possible. Most cowboys also had a set of leather saddlebags, also known as war bags, to accommodate their few personal belongings.

Above: *A variety of classic Western saddles and a saddlebag.*

Of course, the other "equipment" that every cowboy needed was strength of mind and body. The unspoken cowboy code of loyalty, honesty, common sense, and toughness, came to be highly regarded. A true cowboy spoke little, but meant what he said; he was a man who was strong but chose to be gentle. These cowboy virtues have been embodied in many fictional characters, on the page and on screen, and remain powerfully attractive. Perhaps no actor embodied the strong, silent, resourceful Westerner better than John Wayne.

The men often formed life-long friendships out on the prairie, and a distinct cowboy culture grew up around the camaraderie of the campfire. Songs, music, dancing, and poetry all formed a lively counterpoint to their hard and dangerous lives. Many famous cowboy songs date from the heyday of the trail drives and cow camps, and are full of nostalgia, raw sentiment, death, fighting, and humor. The song titles are deeply evocative, and many form a part of country music culture to this day These songs include "The Texas Cowboy," "Blood on the Saddle," "The Old Cow Man," "The Streets of Laredo," "The Call of the Plains," and "The Drunken Desperado."

Below: *A Western saddle blanket in the Navajo style.*

These assorted cowboy verses carry some hint at the different emotions carried by the songs: wistful, tragic, and funny in turns.

I'm wild and woolly and full of fleas,
I'm hard to curry below the knees,
I'm a she-wolf from Shannon Creek,
For I was dropped from a lightening streak
And it's my night to hollow—Whoo-pee!

From "The Drunken Desperado"

There was blood on the Saddle, blood all around
And a great big puddle of blood on the ground
The cowboy lay in it, all covered with gore
Oh pity the cowboy, all bloody and dead
A bronco fell on him and mashed his head.

From "Blood on the Saddle"

Ho! Wind on the far, far prairies!
Free as the waves of the sea!
Your voice is sweet as in alien street
The cry of a friend to me!
You bring me the breath of the prairies
Known in the days that are sped,
The wild geese's cry and the blue, blue sky
And the sailing clouds o'er head.

From "The Call of the Plains"

The spirit of romanticism was one of the strongest surviving elements of the stereotypical aspects of life in the West. Exhibitions like Buffalo Bill Cody's Wild West Show (which ran between 1884 and 1906) celebrated this. The entertainment included a cowboy and Indian battle, a buffalo hunt, and the Deadwood stagecoach. The show also featured real-life Western characters such as Sitting Bull, Wild Bill Hickok, and Annie Oakley. "Pawnee Bill" (Gordon W. Lillie) presented a similar Wild West show between 1888 and 1908.

This idealized view of the cowboy and his skills is still perpetuated by the modern rodeo. Although this form of entertainment now seems like a window into the world of the traditional cowboy, it actually predates Western expansion by over a century. The first rodeos were held in the early 1700s, and celebrated the authentic cowboy chores of tie-down roping, bronc riding (broncs are unbroken horses), and team roping. "Rodeo" was a Spanish vaquero term, meaning "round-up," and did not acquire its modern meaning until 1916. The first "rodeos" were called "Cowboy Competitions," or "Cowboy Tournaments." These included the famous 101 Ranch Wild West Show, founded by Joe Miller in 1905. Brave cowgirls also participated in early rodeos, but the death of the famous Bonnie McCarroll in a 1926 bronc riding accident caused many shows to drop female events. When the Rodeo Association of America was founded in the same year, it was created as an all-male entity.

Originally rodeos were popular with working cowboys as a means of demonstrating their skills, and supplementing their low wages. But participation in the sport has now become a profession in itself. Each year 7,500 contestants compete for over $30 million in prize money, in over 650 American rodeos. Although only loosely based on the folkloric skills of the Western cowboy the modern rodeo still requires extreme courage, strength, and expertise. Many events remain substantially unchanged. These include bull riding (which continues to be the most popular event), steer wrestling, calf roping, and bareback bronc riding. All of these activities are as potentially dangerous as they ever were. There are now several Rodeo Associations that run the sport, and cater for various special interest groups. As a sign of how times have changed, these organizations include the International Gay Rodeo Association, the All Indian Rodeo Cowboys Association, and the Women's Professional Rodeo Association.

Chuck Wagon Western Specialities

Charles Goodnight first introduced the iconic chuck wagon in 1866. Texas rancher, cattle king, and co-founder of the famous Goodnight-Loving trail, Goodnight understood the huge importance that cowhands placed on "larruping good" vittles.

The first chuck wagon was constructed from wood, and drawn by oxen. The chuck box, sited towards the rear of the wagon, had a hinged lid that dropped down to become the food preparation area. The box also contained various drawers and compartments, which held the cooking equipment (Dutch ovens, skillets, and the all-important coffee pot), together with various easily preserved staples such as cornmeal, flour, dry beans, jerky, dried fruit, molasses, coffee, sourdough starter, and chili peppers. Often second only in importance

Below: *Cowboys gather around the chuck wagon at the end of a hard day.*

to the trail boss himself, the chuck wagon "cookie" not only used the materials packed in the wagon, but also foraged for locally available game and produce. Chuck wagon cooks make brief appearances in many Westerns, and are often comedic characters. In John Wayne's 1972 film, *The Cowboys,* "cookie" Jeb Nightlinger is described as a chuck wagon chef, and developed into more of a character.

Unsurprisingly, meat was a large component of the "grease hungry" cowboy diet. Although they had a ready supply of fresh beef, the trail diet was livened up with venison, wild turkey, squirrel, quail, duck, rabbit, and grouse. "Cookie" might also collect herbs (especially sage), acorns, buckwheat, nuts, greens, and wild berries along the trail. By the 1880s, some canned goods were available to chuck wagon cooks on the northern range, including canned tomatoes, peaches, and condensed milk. These luxuries had migrated to the southern range by the 1890s. But although "authentic" chuck wagon recipes sometimes include fresh dairy products and eggs, these were not in general use before the 1920s.

Cowboys often sought to work for the bosses with the best trail cooks, and even described their trail work as "riding the grub line." Western writers, such as Louis l'Amour, were quick to celebrate the mythical powers of chuck wagon cooks to charm the least promising ingredients into appetizing meals. Retired cowboys, who settled down to ranching, missed not only the freedom of the trail, but chuck wagon coffee and biscuits, cooked on an open fire. Equally, less successful cooks were reviled, and heaped with unfriendly epithets, including Belly Cheater, Grub Worm, Gut Robber, and Pot Rustler. While bunkhouse cooks had access to a greater range of equipment and foodstuffs, they could not rival the esteem accorded to a good cook on the open range, Trail bosses rewarded these men with better wages than those of the regular cowboys.

Some cowboy dishes, like "Possum Roast" and "Rattlesnake Soup" may have lost their appeal, but many chuck wagon recipes still sound mighty appetizing. Here are just a few of the most well known.

Below: Chuck wagon coffee served in enamelware.

Chuck Wagon Coffee

Take two pounds of good strong ground coffee. Put in enough water to wet it down. Boil it for two hours, then toss in a horseshoe. If the horseshoe sinks, it ain't ready.

Cowboy Sausages and Sweet Taters

2 pounds of sweet potatoes
½ cup granulated sugar
½ cup brown sugar
¼ cup water

2 tablespoons butter
1 teaspoon salt
1 pound sausages

Set a large pan of water to boil. Parboil the sweet potatoes for 15 minutes. Drain the potatoes, then peel and cut the potatoes into strips. Place them in a greased Dutch oven. Mix the sugars, butter, salt, water, and boil the mixture in a saucepan until thickened slightly. Pour the syrup over the potatoes and bake for around 40 minutes. Place the sausages on top of the potatoes and bake for an additional 30 minutes

Texas Camp Bread
This recipe dates from the 1850s.

10 cups flour
3 teaspoons salt
4 teaspoons black pepper

1 teaspoon sugar
1 tablespoon lard
4 ½ cups water

Sift and mix all the ingredients together. Use lukewarm water to make fairly dry dough. Then let the dough set for 20 to 30 minutes. Roll out the dough until it is ¼ -½ an inch thick. Cut the dough into rounds and cook on a hot, bacon-greased cast iron skillet or Dutch oven. Prink with a fork and turn over when browned on the first side.

Above: *Texas camp bread cooked in an iron skillet.*

Lazy Corn Fritters

1 ¼ cups of flour
2 cups of corn
2 teaspoon baking powder
2 teaspoons salt

½ cup sugar
¼ teaspoon paprika
2 eggs
¼ cup of milk

Mix all the ingredients in a large bowl. Drop spoonfuls of the batter into a large skillet of hot oil, and fry until lightly browned.

THE CHUCK WAGON — THE COWBOYS KITCHEN   TX17

SK3877

Spotted Pup Dessert

1 cup rice
Handful of raisins
1/4 cup molasses

Pinch cinnamon
1 teaspoon vanilla

Above: *"Cookie" works on the hinged lid of the chuck box.*

Put everything in a pot and bring to the boil. Stir the mixture frequently until the water is absorbed by the rice.

Chuck Wagon Beans

1 pound dry pinto beans
Handful bacon or salt pork
1 can tomatoes

1 teaspoon garlic powder
1 teaspoon chili powder
Salt to taste

Pick through the beans to remove any rocks or debris, then rinse them in cold water. Put the beans and pork in a cooking pot and cover them with cold water, two knuckles high above the beans. Cook the beans and pork until they are soft, for around 1 hour 30 minutes to 2 hours. Then add the seasonings and simmer for 30 to 40 minutes to allow the flavors to blend.

Cowboy Beans

2 cups dried red beans
2 cups dried pinto beans
1 chopped onion
3 tablespoons chopped garlic
3 green chili peppers, grilled and diced
3 tomatoes, seeded and chopped
1 tablespoon vegetable oil

7 quarts water or stock
1 smoked ham hock
1 teaspoon toasted coriander
1 bay leaf
2 whole dried red chilies
Salt and pepper to taste

Soak the beans in water overnight, changing the water once. Rinse and drain the beans. Sauté the onions, garlic, green chilis, and tomatoes in oil over medium heat. Add the stock or water and the ham hock, and bring the mixture to boil. Add the beans, coriander, bay leaf, and dried red chilis. Boil for thirty minutes, then lower the heat, cover, and simmer for three to four hours. Check that the beans are tender, then season with salt and pepper to taste. Remove the bay leaf before serving.

Left: A hearty dish of cowboy beans.

Peach Cobbler

On the range, a Dutch oven would be used to cook the cobbler in the campfire, at around 350 degrees.

Above: *A peach cobbler made from tinned fruit, available from the 1880s.*

For the filling:
2 large cans of peaches, undrained
Cinnamon to taste
1 teaspoon vanilla
Sugar to taste

For the topping:
2 cups flour
½ cup sugar
1 teaspoon baking powder
½ teaspoon salt
¼ cup butter
2 to 3 cups of canned milk

Melt the butter in the bottom of the Dutch oven, pour in the peaches, and add the cinnamon and sugar. Cook briefly until the peach syrup thickens slightly. For the topping, put the dry ingredients into a bowl and mix. Add the butter, melted or cold. Add the milk to form a soft ball. Drop small dumpling-sized balls of dough onto the peaches. Sprinkle a little sugar and cinnamon over the mixture. Cover and bake for around 35 to 40 minutes. Lift the lid from time to time to check the progress of the cobbler.

Buffalo Steaks with Chipotle-Coffee Rub

4 buffalo steaks
3 teaspoons ground coffee
3 teaspoons ground chipotle pepper
¼ cup paprika

2 teaspoons toasted cumin seeds
3 tablespoons sugar
1 tablespoon salt

Combine the coffee, chipotle, paprika, cumin seeds, sugar, and salt. Rub the mixture into the buffalo steaks, and then grill the meat until the desired doneness.

Chuck Wagon Stew

2 ½ pounds cubed beef
2 tablespoons all-purpose flour
1 tablespoon paprika
1 teaspoon chili powder
2 teaspoons salt
3 tablespoons lard
2 onions, sliced
1 clove garlic, minced
28-ounce can tomatoes
3 tablespoons chili powder
1 tablespoon cinnamon
1 teaspoon ground cloves
½ teaspoon dry crushed red peppers
2 cups chopped potatoes
2 cups chopped carrots

Coat the beef in a mixture of the flour, paprika, 1 teaspoon of the chili powder, and the salt. Brown the meat in hot lard in a large Dutch oven, then add the onion and garlic and cook until soft. Add the tomatoes, the rest of the chili pepper, the cinnamon, cloves, and crushed red peppers. Cover and simmer for 2 hours. Then add the potatoes and carrots and cook the stew until the vegetables are tender, approximately 45 minutes.

Above: *Chuck wagon stew. Beef was always available.*

Left: *The closed up chuck wagon, ready to roll.*

Jerky

The term "jerky" comes from the method in which the meat is removed from the bones. It was "jerked" away quickly to eliminate most of the sinews. It takes around three pounds of fresh meat to make a pound of jerky.

3 pounds salt
5 tablespoons black pepper
4 tablespoons allspice

Skin one thigh of the animal, muscle-by-muscle, removing the membranes so that only moist flesh remains. Ideally, the pieces of meat should be around 12 inches long, 6 inches wide, and 2 to 3 inches thick. Rub the spice mixture into meat, being sure to cover the meat's entire surface. Hang each piece to dry. If the sun is too hot, hang it in the shade. Never let the meat get even the slightest bit damp. Take it inside if it rains, and cover it with canvas to protect it from the dew. The meat will be at its best after a month.

Missouri Style Barbecued Ribs

The term "3/down" refers to the weight of the ribs. In this case, each rack of 10-12 ribs weighs three pounds or less.

2 tablespoons salt
2 tablespoons chili powder
¼ cup sugar
4 tablespoons paprika
2 tablespoons ground cumin
2 racks of 3/down pork ribs
2 tablespoons fresh ground black pepper

For the basting sauce:
1 ¾ cups white vinegar
1 tablespoon salt
2 tablespoons hot pepper sauce
1 tablespoon ground black pepper
2 tablespoons sugar

Combine the salt, chili powder, sugar, paprika, cumin, and black pepper to make a barbecue rub. Rub the ribs with the mixture, then place them on a baking sheet and bake in a 180 degree oven for three hours. The slow cooking infuses the spices, and there is no need to turn the meat. Remove ribs from the oven. They may now be refrigerated for up to two days. Just before warming to serve, combine the ingredients for the basting sauce. Use a low charcoal fire with the rack as high as possible to grill the ribs on each side until they have a light outer crust and are heated through. For juicy ribs, coat them with the basting sauce before removing them from the grill. Slice ribs in between the bones and serve.

Below: *Cowboys and "Cookie" in their meal break.*

Indian Breakfast

Above: Indian breakfast was a filling start to the day.

15 ounces hominy
1 chopped onion
2 to 3 slices bacon, fried and crumbled

1 bell pepper, finely chopped
Dash cayenne pepper
5 beaten eggs

Sauté the hominy, chopped onion, and bacon in a large skillet. Add the cayenne and bell pepper. Cook for around 10 to 15 minutes on a medium heat. Add the beaten eggs. Stir the eggs gently, and leave the mixture on the heat until they are barely cooked. Serve immediately.

5
The Alamo!

The struggle between Mexico and the Texian settlers ebbed and flowed during the 1830s. In 1835 the Mexican forces were driven out by the Texians and in February 1836 a large force of 1,500 Mexican troops returned to retake the territory. They laid siege to the garrison of Texians at the Alamo, a former Spanish mission in San Antonio. The original garrison of around 100 men had been strengthened by extra men drafted in by the Alamo's commanders James Bowie and William B. Travis. However the resultant defending force of between 181 and 257 men in the flimsily constructed mission was never going to be a match for the Mexican force.

Following a 13-day siege the Mexicans attacked in the early hours of March 6th and after being driven back by the Texians twice, breached the fort's defences on the third attempt. Many of the defenders gained the shelter of the mission's interior rooms but were eventually shot or cut down by Mexican troops and cavalry, including Jim Bowie who was allegedly confined to bed with pneumonia. All but two of the Texian defenders were killed. Santa Anna's perceived cruelty during the battle inspired many Texians—both Texas settlers and adventurers from the United States—to join the Texian Army. Driven by a fierce desire for revenge, the Texians finally defeated the Mexican Army at the Battle of San Jacinto, on April 21, 1836, ending the revolution.

The battle site is now regarded as a potent symbol of American national pride, representing the courage and sacrifice of the founders of the country. This partly explains John Wayne's reasons for making *The Alamo* (1960), which he both starred in and directed.

His avoidance of military service in WWII was a major regret to Wayne after the war. He launched into a series of patriotic movies that projected him as a

Left: *Remember the Alamo! The "Last Stand" defense of the mission fort against overwhelming Mexican forces took place in 1836.*

true American hero. What better vehicle than the Alamo? John Wayne's third wife Pilar Wayne wrote, "He would become a 'superpatriot' for the rest of his life trying to atone for staying home."

When John Wayne appears as Davy Crockett in the movie with his coonskin cap and Kentucky longrifle the audience can be forgiven for thinking that the other 188 or so defenders of the fort were all similarly equipped.

In fact the Alamo was defended by a mixed bunch of men ranging from doctors and lawyers to ranchers and tradesmen. As a result they were armed with what they had, the better-off with imported sporting weapons, the hunter with his rifle, the farmer and tradesman with shotguns.

Previous page: *The preserved part of the front of the fort, which was a former Spanish mission and in reality too frail to stand the repeated attacks of the Mexican forces under Santa Ana.*

Left: *John Wayne as Davy Crockett in the movie* The Alamo *in which he both starred and directed.*

Two forms of gun ignition were available to the defenders in 1836, the flintlock system, which had been around for 200 years and was widely available, and the recently developed percussion cap, which had gained wide usage by the mid 1830s.

The longrifle used by Crockett was developed from the German Jaeger rifle, a design brought to Pennsylvania and Kentucky by German settlers. This type of gun was characterized by its long barrel, rifled for accuracy at long range, and fancy burr walnut or maple stock, often adorned with a patchbox and brass and silver inlaid ornamentation.

Another likely gun in the hands of the defenders was the Plains rifle, a large caliber (usually .58 and above) heavy-barrelled rifle that was usually half-stocked. We show a percussion example here by H. E. Dimick. The Plains rifle was made by gunsmiths in St. Louis, Missouri, that was at one time the "Gateway to the West." They produced what their customers needed in the west, a quality gun, light enough to carry all the time, capable of knocking down big targets at long

Above: *A fine example of full stock Longrifle made by Henry Leman of Lancaster, Pennsylvania. The rifle has a characteristic 39.5-inch barrel and fancy figured maple stock and brass furniture.*

Above: *A classic Plains Rifle by H. E. Dimick of St Louis, Missouri, in .58 caliber with a 32.5-inch barrel.*

range. They called their guns "Rocky Mountain Rifles," reflecting their customers: fur trappers, traders, and explorers.

The Trade rifle was developed for the Indian trade and for bigger game as the settlers moved further west. The fittings of these guns were more spartan with plainer fittings and heavier barrels. They were popular because they were less expensive to buy and were more rugged and practical then the more delicate longrifle. The example here is by Hollis & Sons made for the Hudson's Bay Company.

The detachment of New Orleans Greys that fought at the Alamo was armed with the U.S. Common rifle of 1817. This military rifle was advanced in its use of a paper cartridge and lubed lead ball. We show two examples here. The first is made under contract to the U.S. government by Henry Deringer of Philadelphia. It is a flintlock version with a 33.5-inch barrel in .54 caliber.

The second is also by Deringer and has been converted to the percussion cap system using the "Belgian" method. This is where a piece of brass is inserted into the hole in the lockplate formerly occupied by the flintlock priming pan and frizzen and a percussion nipple is threaded into the barrel vent hole. Both types could well have been in the hands of the Greys.

The Mexican Army had surrendered various of their issue weapons at the Siege of Bexar and these had then fallen into Texian hands. Amongst these were two English manufactured guns. The first was the Baker rifle, designed by Ezekiel Baker and first selected for service in 1800, the Baker was the first general issue rifled weapon to enter British service. A muzzle-loading flintlock piece, it fired a tight-fitting ball which had to be firmly rammed into the barrel. The first soldiers to be issued with the Baker were also given a wooden mallet to help with reloading, although this was soon superseded by the use of a cloth wadding or "patch" to help the ball slide down the barrel. The Baker was used

Above: *An Indian Trade musket specially produced to trade pelts and other valuables from the Indians. The guns were made cheaply and were pretty basic even for the times. This example was made by Hollis & Sons of London for the Hudson's Bay Company.*

Above: *Henry Deringer Sr set up business in Philadelphia in the 1760s and the last government contract he signed before handing over to his son was for 2,000 Model 1814 rifles of the type seen here. The .54 caliber weapon has a 33.5-inch barrel marked "H. Deringer, Philadelphia" and the lock is similarly marked. An unusual feature is the finger ridges on the trigger guard strap.*

Above: *Deringer was one of the companies who won contracts to manufacture the Model 1817 Rifle musket, often known as the "Common Rifle." It is a matter of record that guns of this type were issued to units that fought at the Alamo.*

Above: *A fine example of the British made Baker Rifle, a volunteer model made by Broomhead in London which has a full length stock for use with a sword bayonet.*

Above: *A Brown Bess India Pattern Musket that fought in the American War of Independence. Many such weapons were still in everyday use at the time of the Alamo.*

successfully by British riflemen throughout the Peninsular War and the Waterloo campaign. At this time, riflemen were specialist skirmisher troops, intended to operate in loose, open formations and pick off their targets with aimed fire at longer ranges than possible with smoothbore muskets. The Baker had a lethal range of up to 270 yards. The rifle shown here was a volunteer model made by Broomhead in London, and had the earlier full-length stock for use with the sword bayonet.

The second was the East India Pattern musket or Brown Bess. Surplus guns made for export by the Tower Armouries in London were the standard arms of the Mexican Army. The British East India Company had its own armed forces and armories producing weapons to equip them. When Britain became embroiled in the French Revolutionary Wars the government appealed to the company for weapons. The muskets they supplied became known as the India Pattern, and were a simplification of the current "Brown Bess" design. The Indian Pattern proved to be so effective that British contractors were also encouraged to manufacture this model and it became a standard issue from then on. The one shown here has "9B. ANNAPOLIS.M" stamped in the wooden butt, and was used by the Annapolis Militia during the War of Independence.

The Charleville was another likely contender for use at the Alamo. Vast numbers of this popular military musket, imported into the United States during the War of Independence and from the French Colonies in New Orleans, would have fallen into civilian hands by the time of the Alamo. The first French standardised model musket appeared in 1717, this was followed by a series of major and minor modifications over the ensuing century.

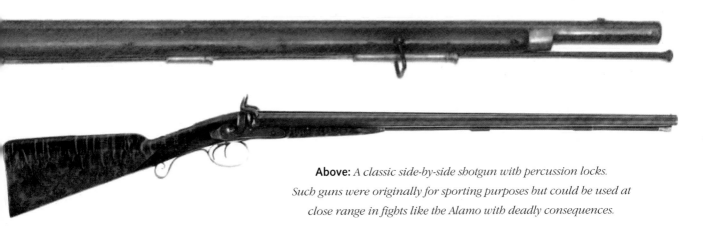

Above: *The French Charleville pattern musket was among weapons supplied by the French to the U. S. Continental Army during the struggle for independence. Like the Brown Bess, its British counterpart, the gun remained in use up to the Alamo.*

Above: *A classic side-by-side shotgun with percussion locks. Such guns were originally for sporting purposes but could be used at close range in fights like the Alamo with deadly consequences.*

The weapon seen above was made in France at the government-owned Manufacture de Charleville with a lock supplied by another of the state arsenals at Maubeuge; three barrel bands suggest that it is either a Model 1728, but it is not a Model 1777 as the priming-pan is made from iron rather than brass. Of much greater significance, however, is that there is very clear evidence from various marks that this was among the weapons supplied to the United States' Continental Army in 1778, during the Revolutionary War. Such French flintlock muskets served as the pattern for the very similar Springfield M1795.

Another useful firearm for close range defence would have been the double-barreled shotgun which William B. Travis himself is known to have favored. He was advocating arming the Texas Army Cavalry with that very weapon. The cavalrymen that he brought with him to the Alamo were almost certainly armed in this way.

The gun shown is from Birmingham (England), manufactured around 1830 but has been imported into the U.S. in parts and stocked by an American gun maker named Skelton in maple. The maple is not a native tree in England.

Pistols were not as common on the frontier as longarms but undoubtedly some would have been used in defence of the Alamo. British horse pistols like the Ketland shown here have a brass barrel, iron mechanism, and walnut stock.

The lock is marked "W/KETLAND/&Co"; it is a complete weapon manufactured by the same company.

Several generations of this family were employed in the weapons business from the mid-eighteenth to mid-nineteenth centuries, based in Birmingham and London. The family also had close ties with the United States and two brothers, John and Thomas Ketland, were resident in Philadelphia from 1797 to 1800 and supplied a large number of weapons to the Commonwealth of Pennsylvania.

American pistols too would have found their way into the hands of the Texians. Guns like the Harpers Ferry Model 1805 would have been in common circulation. The United States government established a southern "Armory and Arsenal" at Harpers Ferry in 1799 to take advantage of the water power supplied by the Potomac and Shenandoah rivers, which meet there. Between 1801 and the outbreak of the Civil War over 600,000 muskets, pistols, and rifles were manufactured, one of the earliest types being

Above: *One of the original cast iron cannon from the siege which is still at the site.*

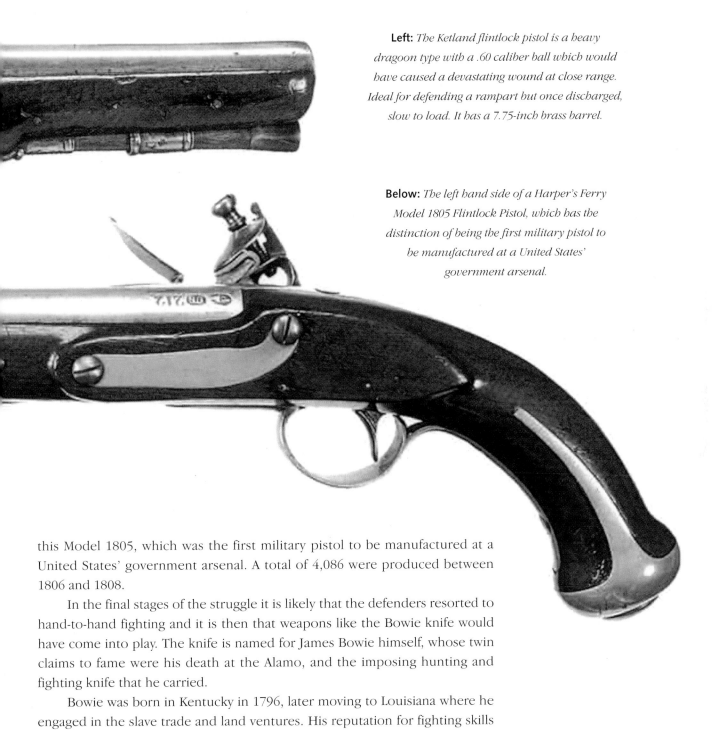

Left: *The Ketland flintlock pistol is a heavy dragoon type with a .60 caliber ball which would have caused a devastating wound at close range. Ideal for defending a rampart but once discharged, slow to load. It has a 7.75-inch brass barrel.*

Below: *The left hand side of a Harper's Ferry Model 1805 Flintlock Pistol, which has the distinction of being the first military pistol to be manufactured at a United States' government arsenal.*

this Model 1805, which was the first military pistol to be manufactured at a United States' government arsenal. A total of 4,086 were produced between 1806 and 1808.

In the final stages of the struggle it is likely that the defenders resorted to hand-to-hand fighting and it is then that weapons like the Bowie knife would have come into play. The knife is named for James Bowie himself, whose twin claims to fame were his death at the Alamo, and the imposing hunting and fighting knife that he carried.

Bowie was born in Kentucky in 1796, later moving to Louisiana where he engaged in the slave trade and land ventures. His reputation for fighting skills stemmed from a legendary brawl in 1827 known as the "Sandbar Fight" in which he finished off his opponent with one thrust of "a large butcher knife." The fame of Bowie and his knife spread and soon men all over the expanding U.S. territories were arming themselves in a similar manner.

Bowie has been the subject of many screen portrayals including being played by Richard Widmark in *The Alamo* (1960) and Scott Forbes in the TV series *The Adventures of Jim Bowie* (1956-58). The knife too, was awarded star status when the Warner Bros. props department created their own rather flashy version with a gold plated back edge to the blade and Jim Bowie's name on a brass plate on the handle, which couldn't have made for a comfortable grip in a tight corner. This version was used in a number of movies including *The Alamo*, Disney's *Davy Crockett*, and the Scott Forbes TV series.

Sadly, reality doesn't always live up to the legend or the Hollywood version, and when Jim Bowie died at the Alamo in the cold dawn of March 6, 1836, he was suffering from pneumonia and probably had little fight left in him as he raised himself from his sickbed to face the onrushing Mexican forces. The legend has him dispatching a dozen enemy soldiers with his trusty blade.

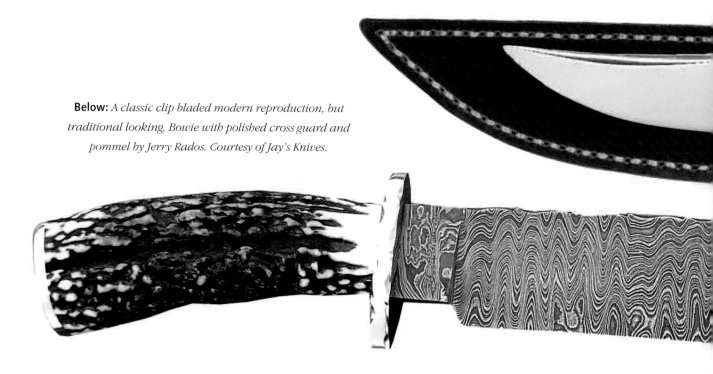

Below: *A classic clip bladed modern reproduction, but traditional looking, Bowie with polished cross guard and pommel by Jerry Rados. Courtesy of Jay's Knives.*

Abovet: *A classic stag handled Bowie with a fine damascened blade from Mooney Custom Knives. The Bowie is still a very popular design for performance fighting knives.*

Abovet: *A vintage handmade Bowie with an 8-inch clippoint blade, coffin-shaped tooled leather grip, and brass pommel.*

Abovet: *A modern stainless steel clip-pointed Bowie with walnut handle, silver pommel and cross guard, and leather sheath.*

6
The Civil War

The *The Horse Soldiers* (1959), directed by John Ford and starring John Wayne as Colonel John Marlowe with William Holden and Constance Towers, is based on the novel by Harold Sinclair of the same name. Sinclair's book takes its inspiration from the true story of Grierson's Raid; a Union cavalry action during the Vicksburg Campaign of the American Civil War, taking place from April 17 to May 2, 1863. Colonel Benjamin Grierson and his 1,700 cavalrymen rode over six hundred miles through enemy territory (from southern Tennessee, through the state of Mississippi, to Union-held Baton Rouge, Louisiana), over routes no Union soldier had traveled before. They destroyed railroad tracks and burned crossties, freed slaves, looted Confederate storehouses, decommissioned locomotives, blew up bridges and trestles, burned buildings, and inflicted ten times the casualties they received, all while detachments of his troops made dummy attacks confusing the Confederates as to his actual whereabouts and direction. The raid was audacious and proved to be extremely successful as well as being relatively bloodless. Only three members of Grierson's force were killed, seven wounded, and nine missing. Five wounded men were left behind needing medical aid. By attacking the

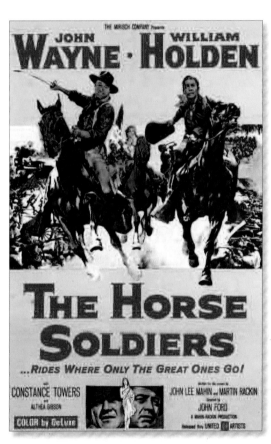

Confederate-controlled railroad it upset the plans and troop deployments of Confederate General John C. Pemberton. Up until this time in the war, Confederate cavalry commanders such as J. E. B. Stuart had outfoxed the Union and it was time to turn the tables. The task fell to Colonel Benjamin Grierson, whose cavalry brigade consisted of the 6th and 7th Illinois and 2nd Iowa Cavalry regiments. Benjamin Henry Grierson (July 8, 1826–August 31, 1911) was a music teacher who hated horses after being kicked in the head by one as a child, strangely becoming a career cavalry officer in the United States Army and later

Left: The real life Horse Soldiers, men of Company I, 5th Ohio Cavalry, proudly display their Sharps breechloading carbines and Model 1860 sabers. Grierson's men would have been similarly equipped.

Below: *A detail of the right side of the lock showing the hammer and pellet priming system which is now integral with the lockplate.*

Above: *A detail of the left side of the straight breech action of the rifle. Note that the original blued finish has mostly been worn away by cleaning.*

Left and below: *The Sharps New Model Carbine viewed from both sides. Note the single band on the 21.5-inch barrel and straight breech action and the sling ring bar extending backwards from the left side of the receiver.*

leading troops in the American Old West. After the Civil War he organized and led the Buffalo Soldiers of the U.S. 10th Cavalry Regiment from 1866 to 1888. The 6th and 7th Illinois and 2nd Iowa Cavalry regiments are known to have been armed with the Sharps new model carbine. Records show that the 2nd Iowa were issued with 226, and the 6th and 7th Iowa with 248 and 399 of these weapons respectively.

The Sharps was a Single shot breechloading percussion carbine developed from an earlier model of the Model 1852. As a result of experience with the Model 1852, the Sharps Company updated the design to what is known as the straight breech, or New Model rifles and carbines. As far as the carbine series goes, some 98,000 were made of Models 1859, 1863, and 1865, although they can be regarded as a single type. The Model 1863, which we are illustrating, was produced both with and without a patchbox (twice as many without). Both our examples are without. They have 21.5-inch barrels and are in the standard .52 caliber.

Above: *The Sharps New Model Rifle shown from both sides. This is a later Model 1865 and part of a contract for the French government but essentially the same gun that saw action in the Civil War. The rapid development in arms technology caused by the needs of the war was recognized by other countries and created a demand for American weapons.*

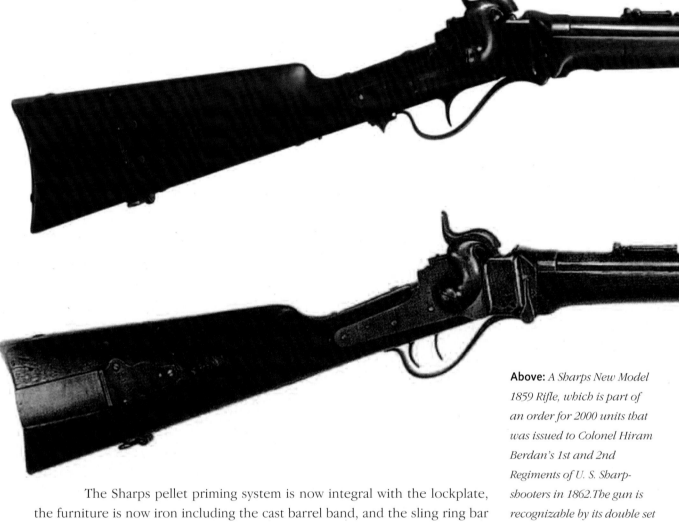

Above: *A Sharps New Model 1859 Rifle, which is part of an order for 2000 units that was issued to Colonel Hiram Berdan's 1st and 2nd Regiments of U. S. Sharpshooters in 1862. The gun is recognizable by its double set trigger modification. It is also notable for its patchbox.*

The Sharps pellet priming system is now integral with the lockplate, the furniture is now iron including the cast barrel band, and the sling ring bar on the left side of the receiver is shorter, extending rearwards to the middle of the wrist. Most of the output was put in the hands of federal troops, but the state of Georgia managed to acquire 2,000 for its cavalry and infantry from the first production of the 1859 model, the only batch to retain brass furniture. A rifle version with double set triggers was developed for use by Berdan's Sharpshooters which had a 30-inch barrel, the same .52 caliber and is also shown here. Ironically, by the time these successful weapons had been developed, Christian Sharps had severed all association with the company, and by 1854 had formed a new partnership with William Hankins.

The other weapon used by the cavalry was the saber:
We had been furnished with sabres before we left Abingdon, but the only real use I ever heard of their being put to was to hold a piece of meat over

Above: *An example of the standard 30-inch barreled New Model Rifle 1859. It has a lug for the saber type bayonet near the muzzle. This one has obviously seen action and was likely part of an order for 1500 rifles for federal army use placed early in the war.*

a fire for frying. I dragged one through the first year of the war, but when I became a commander, I discarded it. Col. John S. Mosby.

In a war where the rifled longarm and explosive shell came to dominate the battlefield, it is ironic that so much effort was put into manufacturing and providing weapons that were anachronistic, obsolete, and of limited value. But both sides continued to make thousands of swords for all kinds of purposes, and to supply every rifleman with a bayonet. Their battle usefulness can be demonstrated in the oft-quoted statistic, where Union hospital records show that only half of one percent of all wounds was caused by sword or bayonet.

The only fighting men that had any real use for a combat sword were the cavalry, although even they saw their pre-war visions of massed charges largely disappear in the face of rifle and artillery fire. Instead, much of their battlefield role became that of mounted infantry, dismounting to fire their carbines from the ground. But occasionally they still did come to saber point, such as at Gettysburg where Confederate Brigadier General Wade Hampton had to fight his way out with sabers when he was cut off by Union troops during an attempt at outflanking the Army of the Potomac.

In the infantry, however, only officers and NCOs were entitled to wear a sword. The latter soon left theirs behind as a useless encumbrance. But the officers kept theirs, more as a badge of rank than as a useful weapon. It did help

Following page: *General William French and his staff pose for a typical "team photograph." Most are carrying Model 1850 Staff and Field Officers swords, intended as a badge of rank rather than a useful military tool.*

to distinguish commanders in action, and a sword held high could be used to signal direction of movement, instructions to fire, or even the location of a rally point in the noise, smoke, and confusion of battle. Senior officers, such as majors and above, had their own patterns of swords, again of mainly symbolic importance, while the wealthier could purchase finely decorated works of art to demonstrate their personal and financial status.

The pre-war Navy had similar obsolete ideas of mass boarding actions being fought, where seaman and officers would wield broad-bladed cutlasses on contested decks. Again, in practice this almost never happened, although a hefty cutlass could be an intimidating tool for Union inspection parties when intercepting vessels suspected of running their blockade of southern ports.

And the truly anachronistic use of edged weapons is demonstrated by the unfortunate Confederate formations who were issued with pikes before their rifles became available, while the 6th Pennsylvania Cavalry rode off to the wrong war with their banners fluttering from their spear like lances. But in the end, the most

Above: *The Model 1860 Cavalry Saber was based on a French design. This example is made by the Ames Manufacturing Company, one of the most prolific American manufacturers of edged weapons. Grierson's men would have carried such weapons.*

Above and left: A Whitney 1861 Navy Percussion (Plymouth Rifle),a typical example of a single shot muzzle loading Civil War rifle complete with Sword bayonet. This was part of a Naval issue when it was envisaged that bayonets would feature in the fighting but in reality it wasn't the case.

common use for the soldier's edged weapon was around camp in the day-to-day tasks of eating, making camp, and making whatever small comforts they could, never mind a sword or bayonet–every soldier needed a knife.

The Ames Model 1860 Cavalry Saber

The Ames Model 1860 Cavalry Saber was intended to replace the earlier Mexican War era Model 1841 cavalry saber. Based on French designs, it was a slightly lighter sword and a little easier to wield on horseback than its predecessor. The sword had a narrow 35-inch blade, only 1 inch wide at the hilt, but as with other swords, there were variations between manufacturers. The handgrip was normally of wood wrapped in leather then wound with twisted copper wire, while the guard was a military pattern three-bar made from brass. The sword shown here is a plain, regulation Model 1860, in a metal scabbard, and made by the Ames

Above: John Wayne as Colonel John Marlowe heads up his cavalry troop in The Horse Soldiers. *Wayne often wore the double-breasted tunic seen here in many cowboy movies.*

Manufacturing Company, the most prolific American manufacturer of edged weapons. The Ames company was started in Cabotville, Massachusetts, by Nathan P. Ames, and began making swords in 1832. Early Ames swords were marked "N. E Ames/Cabotville/Mass". After Nathan died in 1847 the company was continued by his brother James, and markings changed to "Ames Mfg. Co". Cabotville was incorporated into the town of Chicopee in 1848, and the markings on Ames swords were further changed to reflect this. The company rapidly became the most important military sword manufacturer in the United States.

Above: *A pair of well-equipped Union soldiers with Harper's Ferry rifles and sword bayonets. The bayonet mainly found use around camp rather than in action.*

Above: *An early Iron frame Model 1860, one of approximately 400, which were thought to have been made at the Colt Hartford factory. Such models are extremely valuable and are sought after by collectors today.*

Henry Rifle

The antecedent of the famous lever-action Winchester carbine, the Henry rifle, first came into limited military use in the later stages of the Civil War. Despite the undoubted advantage that a 15 shot rifle or carbine would have over the conventional muzzle-loader which most of the troops carried, the Federal Army top brass was slow to recognize its merit. President Lincoln himself endorsed the rival Spencer repeating rifle, test firing it personally, leading to a limited adoption. It was in fact the Navy who were the first customers for the Henry rifle. At those actions where it was used by the Federal infantry, such as the siege of Atlanta later in the war, the gun's prowess was obvious. When the 66th Illinois, armed with Henrys, prevented the numerically superior force of Major General Benjamin F. Cheatham from breaching the Union line around the city, it was because the Confederates had nothing to match their firepower.

In essence, if the Union Army had been equipped with breech loading rifles like the Henry at the outset of the war it is reckoned that the Confederacy would have been beaten within a year.

Invented and patented by B. Tyler Henry (1821-1898), the Model 1860 was chambered for the .44 Henry rimfire cartridge, and had a 15-round, tubular magazine under the barrel. It had an octagonal 24-inch barrel with no foregrip, but with a walnut buttstock and a brass buttplate. Some 14,000 of these rifles were made between 1861 and 1866, of which the early examples had iron frames and the remainder brass frame. When the ring trigger was pushed forward the

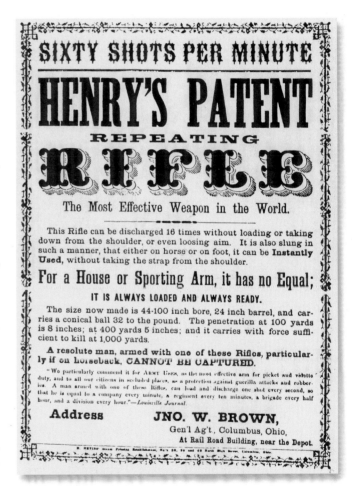

Above: *When it first came out the advantages of owning a Henry were well exploited in the advertising fliers.*

rearmost round in the magazine was forced in to a scoop-shaped carrier by the magazine spring. The hammer was then cocked and the ring trigger drawn to the rear, which lifted the round into the chamber. The Henry rifle represented some very significant advances, the most important being that the 15-round magazine gave the shooter a major increase in firepower. It also, however, suffered from some drawbacks, several of which had tactical implications. The first was that the shooter's forehand held the barrel, which became very hot in a prolonged engagement. The second, and more important, was that the tubular magazine had to be disengaged and reloaded from the front, which meant that the weapon had to be taken out of action and engage the shooter's attention until the task had been completed. Thirdly, the magazine had slots, which allowed dirt to enter.

The company changed its name from the New Haven Arms Company to the Henry Repeating Rifle Company in 1865 and to the Winchester Repeating Arms Company in 1866. This meant that when these problems were overcome in a new model that was introduced that year, it carried the now legendary name of the "Winchester Model 1866."

Previous page: *Co. A, 7th Illinois Color Guard proudly show off their Henry rifles. They were one of few units to be equipped with the rifle during the Civil War.*

Above: *A brass frame Henry serial number 788, which has a homemade rearsight fitted into a slot in the barrel made from an "Indian Head" penny.*

Revolvers

One of the most popular weapons for cavalrymen was a revolver. Two models were preeminent during the Civil War, both Colts. The revolving handgun could be used in close combat with opposition cavalry or fired from horseback into a melee of infantry causing devastating results.

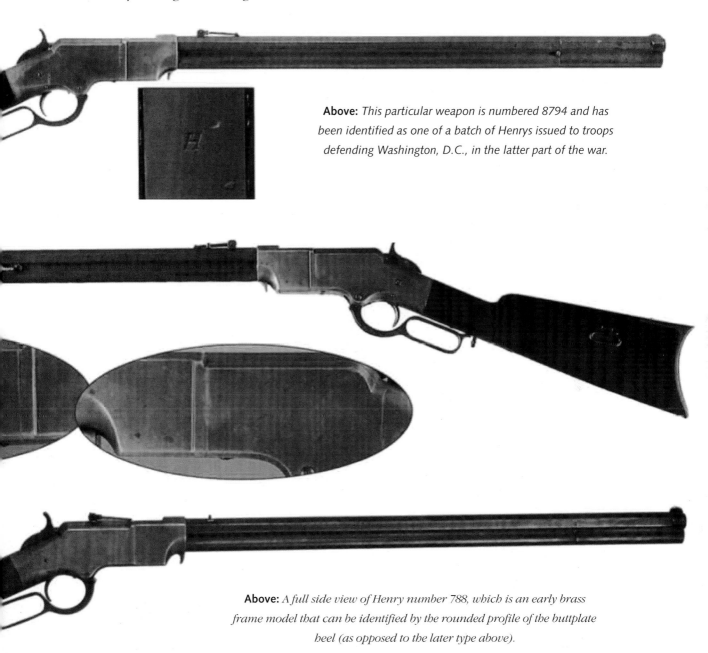

Above: *This particular weapon is numbered 8794 and has been identified as one of a batch of Henrys issued to troops defending Washington, D.C., in the latter part of the war.*

Above: *A full side view of Henry number 788, which is an early brass frame model that can be identified by the rounded profile of the buttplate heel (as opposed to the later type above).*

Colt Model 1860 Army

The production figures for the Colt Model 1860 are self-explanatory, the total produced between 1860 and 1873 was 200,500, of which the U.S. government accepted no less than 127,156. Designed as the successor to the Third Model Dragoon it became one of the most widely used of all handguns during the Civil War and was equally popular in both the Union and Confederate armies.

It was a percussion revolver, with rammer loading from the front of the cylinder and any reasonably experienced shooter ensured that he had a stock of .44 caliber paper cartridges close at hand for rapid reloading. The weapon weighed 2.74 pounds and was fitted with either a 7.5-inch or 8-inch barrel.

Colt Model 1862 Navy

Colt also updated the Model 1851 Navy, using a similar smoothly-shaped barrel and rammer shroud to that of the Model 1860 Army. The ensuing design is an elegant and visually appealing weapon with a 7.5-inch barrel and a smooth-sided cylinder housing six .36 caliber shots. Some 39,000 were made, and through its lifetime there were remarkably few variations on the Model 1861.

Left: *Sergeant Stephen Clinton (right) poses with a comrade from the Sixth Virginia Cavalry. Clinton has a large Colt .44 Army revolver in his belt, while the second man has a smaller Colt, probably a Model 1849.*

Right: *This Model 1861 is accompanied by what would appear to be its original black leather holster, although it has not stood the test of time so well as the gun.*

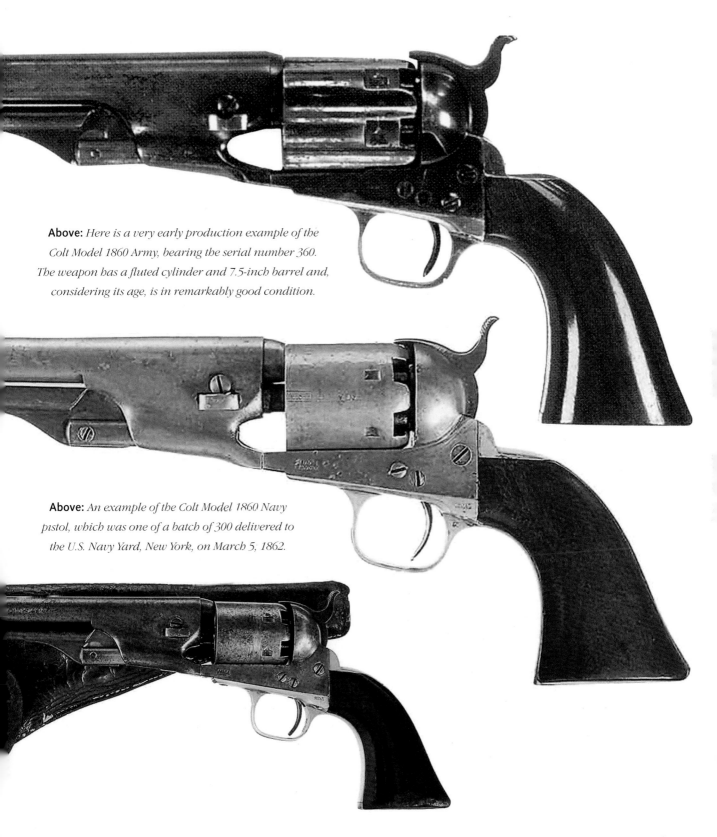

Above: *Here is a very early production example of the Colt Model 1860 Army, bearing the serial number 360. The weapon has a fluted cylinder and 7.5-inch barrel and, considering its age, is in remarkably good condition.*

Above: *An example of the Colt Model 1860 Navy pistol, which was one of a batch of 300 delivered to the U.S. Navy Yard, New York, on March 5, 1862.*

7
The Indian Wars

The Indian Wars began with the Pequot War of 1637 and persisted through many waves of violence to the Wounded Knee massacre of 1890, and the "closing" of the American frontier. Hostilities did not completely stop until the early years of the twentieth century. Essentially, these conflicts were fought to "free" Native American lands for settlement. There was terrible bloodshed on both sides in fighting and warfare, but many women and children were also killed in frontier massacres. Scholars estimate that at least 45,000 Indians and 19,000 whites were killed between 1850 and 1890 alone. Although Native American tribes waged war at a mostly tribal and local level, tribes also formed alliances (such as the Iroquois Confederation) to ward off the unwelcome incursion of European settlers into their lands. Perhaps the most intense fighting took place west of the Mississippi during and after the Civil War. This was largely because this was the most active period of Western expansion. The action of the fighting took place in several theaters of war. Hostilities were waged against Kiowa, Comanche, Sioux, Cheyenne, Arapaho, Ute, Shoshone, Paiute, Bannock, Northern Shoshone, Navajo, Apache, Modoc, Nez Perce, Sioux, and the Dakota all over the region. Hotspots included the Great Plains, the Rockies, the Great Basin, California, the Pacific Northwest, Texas, Dakota, and New Mexico.

The Pike's Peak Gold Rush of 1859, the Black Hills Gold Rush of 1875 to 1878, and the Montana Gold Rush of 1862 to 1863 all brought an uncontrolled flood of immigrants to the West, and led to a substantial increase in tension. Large-scale ranching and the enclosure of tribal lands for grazing also resulted in conflict. The development of new trails (especially the Oregon and California Trails) and Mormon immigration to Utah also

Left: *Yellow Shirt, a Sioux warrior, holding the sacred Horse Dance Stick.*

Below: *Sitting Bull, leader of the Hunkpapa Sioux.*

PACIFIC OCEAN

TLINGIT

NORTH WEST COAST CULTURE AREA

GROS VENT

FLATHEAD

NEZ PERCE

CAYUSE

BLACKFOOT

PLATEAU CULTURE AREA

SHOSHONI

MODOC

THE GREAT BASIN

PENUTIAN FAMILY

UTE

CALIFORNIAN INDIAN CULTURE AREA

PAIUTE

GRAND CANYON

HOPI

NAVAJO

PUEBLOS

MOHAVE

ZUNI

TONTO

MESCALE

SOUTH WEST INDIAN CULTURE AREA

PAPAGO

APAC

WOODED AREAS

PLAINS - LONG GRASS

PLAINS - SHORT GRASS

SAGE BRUSH - SEMI DESERT

DESERT - SCRUB VEGETATION - CACTUS

MILES 0   100   200   300

BEFORE THE COMING OF THE WHITE MAN

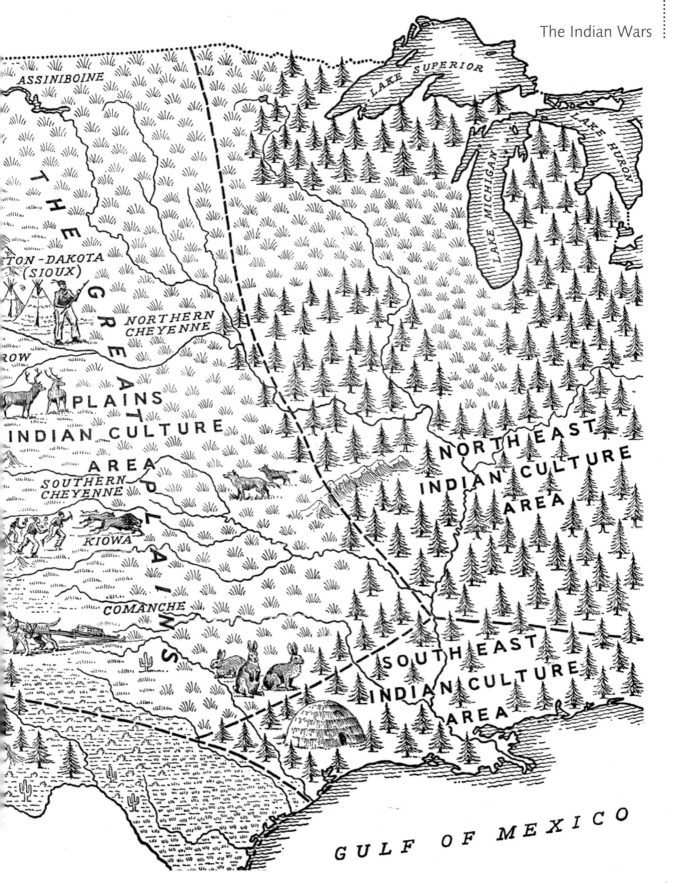

ASSINIBOINE

THE

GREAT

TON-DAKOTA
(SIOUX)

NORTHERN
CHEYENNE

ROW

PLAINS

INDIAN CULTURE

AREA

SOUTHERN
CHEYENNE

KIOWA

COMANCHE

PLAINS

LAKE SUPERIOR

LAKE MICHIGAN

LAKE HURON

NORTH EAST

INDIAN CULTURE

AREA

SOUTH EAST

INDIAN CULTURE

AREA

GULF OF MEXICO

impacted the previously friendly relations with the local tribes, as the area's natural resources came under increased pressure. White incomers, like the Mormons, often secured the most fertile land for themselves, without compensating the Indians they displaced. The generally powerless Native Americans sometimes resorted to violence to try and discourage white settlement. This led to brutal reprisals and a general sentiment in favor of Indian removal. The brutality of the encounters between whites and Indians increased as the 1860s and 1870s progressed, until peaceful relationships between the two groups became impossible.

During the Civil War period, Federal Army units had been withdrawn from the region to fight the Confederate forces in the East. They were replaced by volunteer infantry and cavalry regiments that were drawn from the Territorial governments of the West, and local militias. These men were so effective that they held the West for the Union, defeating the incursions of Confederate forces into New Mexico, and delivered the region to the post-war U.S. government. At this point, many veteran troops, released from the fighting of the Civil War, returned to the region and joined the security forces. This can also be said to have fuelled the fighting in the West.

Culturally, the Indian Wars had a huge impact on the history and legend of the West. John Ford's "Cavalry Trilogy" of films, starring John Wayne, was released between 1948 and 1950. They revolve around real historical events, and shed an interesting contemporary light on them.

Cavalry Regiments of the Indian Wars

The 7th United States Cavalry was undoubtedly the most famous regiment to fight in the Indian Wars. Constituted in 1866 the regiment was made up of twelve companies. Like most of the post war cavalry, its troops were armed mainly with single-action Colt .45 revolvers and modified single-shot .50 caliber Model 1865 Spencer carbines. These were based on the Spencer Model 1863 of the early Civil War era, but had shorter, 20-inch barrels. These guns were finally replaced by the Springfield Model 1873, beginning in 1874. Although sabers were still issued, these were now largely ceremonial. Following a pattern familiar in the West, the 7th was based at Fort Riley in Kansas until 1871, where its mission was to enforce United States law in the subjugated South.

But the regiment was also involved in anti-Indian action, including the famous 1868 Battle of Washita River. Commanded by General Custer, the 7th attacked Chief Black Kettle's Cheyenne village. Even at the time, Custer's attack on a sleeping village was controversial. The general was accused of sadism and his men of killing women and children indiscriminately.

Both above: *Sioux Chief Iron Tail, survivor of Wounded Knee. A Cheyenne warrior in war bonnet with ermine drops and beaded brow band.*

In 1873, the 7th U.S. Cavalry moved its base to Fort Abraham Lincoln in Dakota Territory. The regiment's initial brief was to reconnoiter, and map the Black Hills mountain range, which stretches between South Dakota and Wyoming. Custer's discovery of gold in the Black Hills, during his expedition of 1874, had a profound effect on the region. Not only did this discovery precipitate the huge social upheaval of the Gold Rush, but it also exacerbated conflict with the Sioux, Lakota, and Cheyenne tribes, who were under the leadership of Sitting Bull and Crazy Horse. Modern historians accuse President Grant of deliberately provoking war with the native peoples; he was desperate for gold-fueled growth to lift the economy out of depression.

But victory against the Sioux and Cheyenne peoples was only achieved at a huge cost to the men of the 7th cavalry. The Battle of Little Bighorn (June 25 to June 26, 1876), also known as Custer's Last Stand, saw 52 percent of the regiment fall. The final half hour of the engagement resulted in the deaths of 210 cavalrymen (258 perished all together). These included Custer himself, two of his brothers (Captain Thomas Custer and their youngest brother, civilian scout

Below: *Custer's 7th Cavalry forces ride to Little Bighorn in 1876.*

Above: *Springfield Model 1873 recovered from the battlefield of Little Bighorn.*

Left: *Postcard depicting Custer's Last Stand.*

Below: *John Wayne in* She Wore a Yellow Ribbon.

and forage master, Boston Custer), and the Custers' nephew, Autie Reed. This rout occurred because of a highly ill-advised decision on the general's part to mount an attack on an Indian village in the Montana Territory. Every man and horse of the 7th that fought at Little Bighorn perished at the scene. The single exception was Captain Keogh's famous mount, Comanche.

Custer's Last Stand was the most devastating defeat ever suffered by the United States Cavalry, but the General's reputation remained strangely unstained, largely due to the efforts of his widow Elizabeth Bacon Custer and Buffalo Bill Cody. Although many commentators now place this cataclysmic defeat at Custer's feet, others point out that, by the time it took place, many cavalry recruits were malnourished and ill-trained immigrants from Ireland, England, and Prussia.

John Ford's first "Cavalry Trilogy" movie, *Fort Apache,* is set in the immediate post-Civil War period, and is loosely based on the events of Custer's Battle of Little Bighorn, and the Fetterman Massacre of 1866. All three movies in this trilogy were based on

stories by James Warner Bellah. In this first film, Wayne plays the highly regarded veteran, Captain Kirby Yorke, who is based at Fort Apache, under the command of Lt. Colonel Owen Thursday. Thursday's complete mishandling of the Indians (Apaches in the film, Sioux in the real battles) leads to a bloody rebellion in which most of the garrison is wiped out. Believing him to be an honorable man, the Apaches spare Yorke, and he survives to command the regiment. Apart from the historical elements of the film, it is also interesting for being the first movie to show Native Americans in a sympathetic light.

This chapter in the Indian Wars was brought to a somewhat ignominious close. Crazy Horse was promised a reservation for his weary and starving people, but this never materialized. Ultimately, a soldier bayoneted Crazy Horse to death, as he tried to evade imprisonment.

Above: *John Wayne and his mentor, John Ford, the iconic movie director.*

Several other United States Cavalry regiments fought extensively in the Indian Wars.

The 4th United States Cavalry was formed in 1855, and deployed to Texas after the war. Its main duties there were to protect settlers and the U.S. mail from Indian attack. In 1871 the regiment was called to more active duties, protecting the Texas frontier from Comanche and Kiowa attack. In March 1873, a large part of the regiment was transferred to Fort Clark, from where they made forays into Mexico to prevent highly destructive Apache raids into Texas. In 1880, the 4th was transferred to Arizona Territory, still pursuing their nemesis, the Apache. Six years later, in 1886, the 4th was instrumental in the capture of Geronimo. In 1890, the troops of the 4th were redeployed to Washington State, and took no further part in the Indian Wars. Over the period of their involvement, the regiment had had many successes against a number of Indian tribes, including the Comanches, Kiowas, Quahadi, Kotsoteka, Cheyennes, and Apaches.

The third film in John Ford's "Cavalry Trilogy," *Rio Grande* (1950), is set in post-war Texas, where the cavalry are deployed to protect white settlers from Apache attack. It focuses on Kirby Yorke's later cavalry career. Wayne's character is now a Lt. Colonel, posted to the Texas Frontier to defend the state's new settlers. Ordered by his former Civil War commander to cross the Rio Grande to chase the Apache raiders into Mexico, Yorke faces a court marshal and dishonor if his mission is unsuccessful. In many ways, this is a more conventional movie than *Fort Apache*. The movie's Native American characters are shown as far less compassionate and more brutal (they capture a wagonload of evacuated children to use as hostages). The action of the film is also more predictable; Wayne rescues the children and leads his cavalry in a full-scale attack on the Apache

Above: *Custer with Indian scouts and his favorite Remington.*

Far left: *A studio photograph of Sitting Bull and Buffalo Bill. Sitting Bull was one of the major attractions in Cody's Wild West Show.*

Left: *Apache scouts in Arizona, 1871.*

Above: *A Burnside carbine.*

Far left: *A second lieutenant of the 1st and 2nd Dragoons.*
Middle: *Nathan Bedford Forrest, cavalry officer.*
Above: *A Federal cavalryman of the Civil War period.*

The 5th United States Cavalry was raised in Louisville, Kentucky, in 1855, and was originally designated the 2nd United States Cavalry Regiment. In 1861, this regiment split between men loyal to the Confederacy and those who supported the Union. The Union cavalrymen were re-designated as the 5th, and these men were instrumental in saving their artillery at the Battle of Gaines' Mill in 1862. In the postbellum Plains Indian Wars, the regiment's main duty was to recapture escaped Sioux and Cheyenne and repatriate them to their reservations. They were also instrumental in the defeat of the Miniconjou Sioux at the Battle of Slim Buttes, which took place in Dakota Territory in 1876. Colonel Wesley Merritt led the troops in this engagement. This victory was of huge psychological importance, as it was the first significant defeat of the tribes since the annihilation of Custer's 7th.

The 6th United States Cavalry, the "Fighting Sixth," also took a major part in the Indian Wars. It was raised in 1861, and became part of the Union Army of the Potomac during the Civil War. Between 1865 and 1871, the regiment was

deployed in the Reconstruction of Texas. The regiment also fought in the Indian Wars, and clashed with Geronimo and his Apache braves on more than one occasion.

The 8th Cavalry Regiment was formed in 1866, and organized at Camp Reynolds, Angel, California. Unsurprisingly many of its recruits were "forty-niners" and were reputed to be pretty wild characters. The regiment's first duties were to protect the settlers and travelers of Nevada, Colorado, Arizona, and New Mexico from opportunistic attacks from Apache and Navajo tribesmen. They often provided armed escorts. The 8th also fought in the Apache Wars of southern New Mexico, and engaged with warriors from the Navajo, Comanche, and Kiowa tribes. As more settlers moved into the Northwestern states, the 8th also undertook the longest-ever cavalry march in May, 1885: 2,600 miles to their two new regimental headquarters at Ford Meade, South Dakota, and Fort Keogh, Montana.

In the postbellum era of the United States Cavalry, the force focused its attention on the American interior. Many of the native peoples were now confined to reservations, and a main focus of the cavalry's mission was keeping

Above right: *A cavalryman in front of a native village.*

Above left: *A sergeant in the 5th or 6th Michigan cavalry.*

Left and below: *The U.S. cavalry on practice exercise.*

Right: *Chief Geronimo, the famous Apache warrior.*

them there. In the second movie of John Ford's "Cavalry Trilogy," *She Wore a Yellow Ribbon* (1949), John Wayne plays an aging U.S. Cavalry Captain, Nathan Cutting Brittles, based at Frontier Fort Starke. The movie is set just after Custer's cataclysmic defeat at the Battle of Little Bighorn (1876), and Brittles's final mission is to deal with a breakout of Cheyenne and Arapaho braves. Despite the movie's shallow tagline, "Wayne's greatest role as an Indian fighting Captain!" most of the action actually concentrates on his efforts to prevent a widespread outbreak of hostilities, and his attempts to negotiate peace with Chief Pony that Walks (played by real-life Chief John Big Tree). The film focuses on Brittles's revulsion at the bloodshed that has taken place, and his determination to prevent further loss of life.

Left: *U.S. Cavalry enlisted man's uniform of the 1870s.*

Right: *U.S. Cavalry officer's uniform of the Indian Wars period.*

U.S.

Cavalry Apparel

Cavalry regiments stationed on the Frontier often adopted items of Western garb, in response to the prevailing conditions. The flamboyant General Custer and his officers (including his brother Tom Custer, and Captains Cook and Keogh) were famous for wearing an "undress" cavalry uniform of their own invention. This consisted of fringed buckskin jackets and trousers, buckskin gauntlets, broad-brimmed scouting hats, and long leather riding boots. The group was probably dressed like this when they perished at Custer's Last Stand.

Above: *U.S. Cavalry enlisted man's hat of the 1870s with acorn tassels.*

Many enlisted men bought their own shirts and handkerchiefs, carrying their standard issue dark blue blouses rolled up on their saddles. By the 1880s, the field uniform had somewhat adapted to the conditions of the West, but the dress uniform introduced in 1882 was extremely elaborate. Based on contemporary Prussian cavalry attire, it was festooned with braid, tassels, and gilt buttons. Needless to say, this was not designed for field use.

left: *Confederate cavalry officer's coat, 1861.*

Civilian cavalry scouts, who were often Native Americans of the Seminole or Apache tribes, also had a kind of uniform. This was often a hybrid of the cavalry uniform (the dark blue jacket) and native dress. Apaches in particular often wore a head-band, and red was their favored color. In 1890, the cavalry authorized a special badge to be worn by their scouts; this consisted of

Below: *Detail of U.S. cavalry trousers.*

COL. W. F. CODY. "BUFFALO BILL."

Stacy

WILD WEST

CORNER
9TH ST. & 5TH AVE.
BROOKLYN.

Left: Jenny LaPointe made these Lakota Sioux moccasins.

Left: *Buffalo Bill served as the chief scout for the 5th cavalry.*
Right: *Custer in his undress cavalry uniform of fringed buckskin.*

crossed arrows in nickel, with red and white cords. Rank chevrons were also authorized for the Indian scouts.

Buckskin gloves became particularly popular with cavalrymen. They were soft and comfortable, while still offering good protection to the hands and wrists. They were often beaded, embroidered, or fringed. Native American craftsmen and women (particularly from the Nez Perce tribe) sold thousands of pairs of carefully crafted buckskin gloves to the cavalry.

While John Wayne wears a readily identifiable United States Cavalry uniform in several films, and especially Ford's "Cavalry Trilogy," he never attires himself in the foppish style favored by Custer.

175

8
Classic Western Characters

Gamblers and Gambling in the West

"I assert, without fear of successful contradiction from those who know, that not one professional gambler in a thousand is at all times absolutely square." From *Easy Money* by Harry Brolaski, 1911

Among the many types of men and women who came west to exploit other westerners, the gamblers were some of the most colorful. Gambling reflected the very character of the region, with its willingness to take chances and its spirit of reckless adventure. A mania for gambling was common to all the frontier regions, and it was the chief draw of saloon life. Most gamblers were parasitic and migrated to wherever there was money. Towns like Abilene tried to control the activities of the "pasteboard pirates" with a stringent system of fines, but the town's own Marshal, Bill Hickok, was a professional gambler who ran the town from a saloon table. Bat Masterson wrote, somewhat ironically, that "gambling was not only the principle and best-paying industry of the town at the time, but it was reckoned among the most respectable." Indeed, *The Abilene Chronicle* published a whole list of well-known card tricks employed by cheats and "short-card artists" for their more respectable readers to watch out for.

Almost every Western movie shows men, and occasionally ladies, playing cards, roulette, or other games of chance.

The classic Western movie star, John Wayne, was a lifelong gambler and poker player, and gaming and boozing were key components of his adult social life. He and his movie director friend, John Ford, formed the famous "Young Men's Purity, Abstinence and Snooker Pool Association," a club of actors, writers, and directors who liked to drink and play poker together. The "guys" included Montgomery Clift, Maureen O'Hara, and Dean Martin. After an all-night poker game with a Hollywood animal trainer, Wayne famously won "all the Lassies" (according to his wife, Pilar), but generously returned the dogs to their owner. When he was down, his gambling could become obsessive. After his divorce from Pilar in 1973, a friend remembered how Wayne had lost $11,000 on one roll of the dice in Vegas.

Above: *Bat Masterson of the Dodge City Gang.*

Left: *N. C. Wyeth's painting of Bill Hickok exposing a cheat at cards.*

As the rest of America became less tolerant of gambling and other forms of "vice" many professional gamblers made a strategic move west. Their first targets were the Mississippi riverboats, and it is estimated that between six and seven hundred "gamesmen" worked the boats in the 1840s. Famous gamblers, like Charles Cora, made huge fortunes on the river. Notorious as the Mississippi's foremost faro player, Cora was reputed to have won over $85,000 in six months. Riverboat gamblers Jimmy Fitzgerald and Charles Starr were equally renowned for their sartorial elegance. The originators of the riverboat gamblers' sharp dress code; the pair was always the epitome of good style. They sported expensive black suits and boots, ruffled white shirts, brocaded vests, conspicuous jewelry, and silver-topped walking canes. But as the riverboats gave way to the railroads, the gamblers moved into the West to ply their trade.

In the 1942 film, *Lady for a Night*, John Wayne's character, Jackson Morgan, is a swell river gambler, engaged to river boat owner Jenny Blake. Together, the pair run a lucrative business dedicated to water-borne pleasure; drinking, gambling, dancing, and women. Ironically, Morgan is sacrificed to Blake's social ambitions, as she yearns to leave her flamboyant past behind. Jackson Morgan was a close portrait of real-life riverboat gamblers, like George Devol, the author of *Forty Years a Gambler on the Mississippi*. In the course of his working life, Devol was involved in endless skirmishes. He wrote that he had been "struck some terrible blows

on my head with iron dray-pins, pokers, clubs, stone-coal and bowlders." He survived to win over 2 million in his playing career. But like so many gambling fortunes, Devol's money melted away like snow, and he died penniless. Easy come, easy go.

The California Gold Rush initiated a massive gambling boom on the West Coast, and San Francisco took over from New Orleans as America's gaming capital. The Barbary Coast area of the city became a red-light district replete

Above: *Two fine riverboats, used as floating gambling dens.*

with all the forbidden pleasures, especially gambling and prostitution. The massive influx of gold money into the city meant that the 1850s and 1860s were the Golden Age of gambling in California. Fortunes in gold dust changed hands daily. The city's Portsmouth Square was the epicenter of the trade, and was ringed with popular gaming establishments. The Parker House was the most notorious of these gambling dens. It was said that over half a million dollars was won there nightly. This establishment was flanked by two equally flamboyant enterprises, Samuel Dennison's Exchange and the El Dorado Gambling Saloon.

The Flame of the Barbary Coast (1945) recreates the area brilliantly. John Wayne plays Montana cowboy, Duke Fergus. Almost inevitably, the innocent Fergus is seduced by Ann Tarry, the star attraction of the finest gambling hall in town, and the eponymous "Flame." After being initially fleeced, Fergus turns to professional gambling to impress her and becomes a poker genius, beating every casino champion on the Barbary Coast. Ultimately, he is so successful that he builds his own opulent gambling hall.

Violence and criminality flourished in the wake of the gambling industry, and the citizens of San Francisco became increasingly intolerant. Ultimately, the townsfolk lynched several card sharks. The State of California finally outlawed gambling in the 1890s. Feeling unwelcome, the gamblers followed the money to

Above: *Faro was a popular Western game of chance.*

Left: *Frontier gold miners seeking their fortune.*

the region's mining and cow towns. Miners and cowhands rolled into saloons all over the West with cash and gold dust burning holes in their jeans, and soon became prey.

Unsurprisingly, not all "games" were on the level. A whole industry had sprung up to help professional card sharks fleece money from the gullible by manufacturing "gaffed" equipment. This included "advantaged cards," loaded dice, rigged roulette wheels, and faro layouts.

The Western gambling boom spawned any number of colorful characters, both male and female. Many professional gamblers were also gunmen, from both sides of the law.

One of the most famous of these was Wild Bill Hickok, who ended his wide-ranging career as a professional gambler. The barrier between the law and gambling was often permeable. In *Dakota* (1945), Wayne plays a professional gambler, John Devlin, who ultimately throws in his lot with the Dakota wheat farmers to help them save their land from swindling "entrepreneurs." Hickok himself went the other way. Always irascible, he famously shot Dave Tuff to death when he was unwise enough to beat him at cards. In fact, Hickok was generally too drunk to be a successful player, and often took his winnings by violence rather than skill. In his final years, Hickok hurtled down a desperate spiral of drink, depravity, and violence. Ultimately, he himself was shot to death while playing cards in Deadwood. His assassin was his fellow card shark, Jack McCall. As he died, Hickok held the now legendary "Dead Man's Hand": the ace of spades, the ace of clubs, the eight of clubs, the eight of spades, and the queen or jack of diamonds.

Above: *"Doc" Holliday, famous gambler and gunfighter.*

One of the few Western gamblers to die in his bed, Dick Clark was also one of the most successful. He plied his trade in the traditional gambling towns of Tombstone and Deadwood, and became the owner of the Alhambra Saloon and Gambling Hall. Card playing partner of Wyatt Earp, Clark became known as the "King of Gamblers," and inspired a generation of younger men. He died of tuberculosis in 1893.

Luke Short was one of Dick Clark's protégés. Short worked for Wyatt Earp in Tombstone's famous Oriental Saloon. He opened his own establishment, the famous Elephant Saloon in Fort Worth, Texas, which became a haunt of the most famous Western cardsharps. The Elephant hosted some of the era's most famous card games, whose players included Bat Masterson, Wyatt Earp, and Charlie Coe.

Soapy Smith was one of the gambling brotherhood's less reputable characters. Known as the "King of the Frontier Con Men," he was known for his motto, "Get it while the gettin's good." Like many of his type, Soapy was also an argumentative drunk who provoked the wrong man once too often. Fatally shot by the equally unpleasant Frank Reid, his last words are said to have been, "My God, don't shoot."

Thrown onto their own resources, several well-known Western women also took to the gaming tables, and their success often surpassed that of their male counterparts.

Lottie Deano inherited her love of gambling from her father. When her family sent her, unaccompanied, to Denver to find a suitable husband, she ran off with a highly unsuitable jockey, Johnny Golden. Golden proved his low caliber by introducing his young wife to riverboat gambling. But Lottie soon demonstrated her extraordinary ability. When the couple split, she became the house gambler at San Antonio's University Club, and earned her moniker, the "Queen of the Pasteboards." Ultimately, Lottie married a wealthy banker and became a society woman. She is immortalized as *Gunsmoke*'s Miss Kitty.

"Big Nose" Kate, Doc Holliday's common-law wife, made the career change from prostitution to card shark at his insistence. Having met in Bessie Earp's "sporting house," the pair traveled the West as professional card sharks, specializing in blackjack.

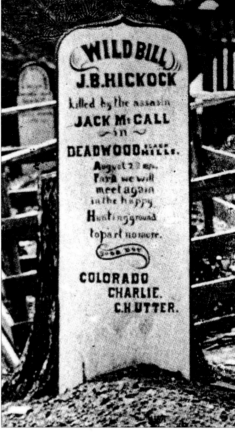

Above: *Hickock's tombstone in Deadwood cemetery.*

Left: *A cheat's top hat, with a mirrored crown.*

A better-looking woman, Poker Alice, used her feminine charms to mesmerize her fellow players. Born Alice Ivers, Poker Alice also came into the gambling trade through the influence of her husband. As a mining engineer, Frank often visited the camp "parlors" in company with his wife. Fascinated by the card play, Alice joined in, and proved herself extremely able. When Frank was killed in a mining accident, Alice supported herself by playing poker and earned her famous nickname. She worked in gambling halls across Colorado, Oklahoma, and New Mexico, and earned a fortune, of up to $6,000 a night. Ultimately, Alice opened a brothel and became famous for her trademark cigar.

Kitty LeRoy was another famous female gambler, equally notorious as a bad-tempered shootist. Five times married, Kitty was the proprietor of Deadwood's Mint Gambling Saloon. Having shot at least one husband to death, Kitty met her own demise at the hands of husband number five. The man had taken issue with her rekindled romance with husband number three. She was only twenty-eight when she died, following a short, but colorful, life.

As the West became more civilized, its citizens became tired of the explosive cocktail of gambling, drink, and vice that had resulted in so much violence, death, and disorder. Its townsfolk longed for the well-regulated and peaceful life typical of the East. Many states and cities had outlawed gambling by the 1890s, and it was gradually driven into smaller and smaller enclaves across the West. The days of the professional gambler were gradually numbered, and few were nostalgic for the old days. Despite this, some Westerners were aware that the gradual control of gambling was symbolic of the loss of the untrammeled freedom of the frontier. It was a sign that the region was being gradually tamed, and becoming just like everywhere else.

Saloon Chanteuses and Soiled Doves

"Ah women! I never met one yet that was half as reliable as a horse!"
John Wayne as Sam McCord in *North to Alaska* (1960)

It soon became apparent that Western morals were different. The Gold Rush attracted huge numbers of single men to the West, and they were soon in desperate need of "entertainment" and female company.

Saloon and dance hall girls were virtually unknown in the East, but they became an integral and celebrated part of Western life. This is hardly surprising, as men outnumbered women three-to-one in most camps and frontier towns. Saloon girls also pepper John Wayne's Western films. The line between saloon girl and prostitute is often quite blurred, with very little open eroticism shown.

Above: *More fortunes were made kitting out the miners than from gold mining.*

These women are almost always portrayed as beautiful and sassy, and most have the proverbial heart of gold.

In the California Gold Rush of the 1850s, men formed 90 percent of the population, and "working girls" were even more highly valued. Unsurprisingly, gold miners became notorious for their generosity. As the well-known prostitute Diamond Toothed Gerty remarked, "The poor ginks have just

Above: *A woman drinking beer in 1898.*

185

gotta spend it. They're that scared they'll die before they have it all out of the ground." Some miners were completely cleaned out by unscrupulous women and went back to the goldfields empty-handed.

Anxious to cash in on the booming economy of the West, saloon and dance hall owners lured attractive girls away from farms or mills. The more glamorous work they offered paid around $10 per week, plus commission on the over-priced drinks they sold to the customers. The girls dressed in brightly colored,

ruffled dresses, with outrageously short skirts, net stockings, and garters. More controversially, they also wore makeup, dyed their hair, and carried concealed weapons. But these "hostesses" were highly valued by the male customers, and many were lavishly rewarded for their company. In *Old California* (1942), Lacey Miller (Binnie Barnes) is an archetypal saloon songstress in a Gold Rush town, livening the house with a rousing chorus of "California Joe." Lacey's relationship with her employer, Albert Dekker, is true-to-life ambiguous. Is she his mistress or just an employee? He certainly resents her attraction to John Wayne's character, Tom Craig, the mild-mannered druggist from Boston.

The West was soon thick with thousands of saloons. Most of these establishments sold their own particular concoction of "Firewater" whiskey, which might have contained raw alcohol, burnt sugar, chewing tobacco, turpentine, ammonia, gun powder, and/or cayenne in its list of ingredients. Saloons also served warm beer.

The first Western dance hall opened in 1849, and others opened almost immediately after. Most of the early customers were gold miners, who paid for

Above: *Crapper Jack's Dance Hall in Cripple Creek, Colorado.*

their pleasures with pinches of gold dust. Men paid the equivalent of between 75 cents and a dollar for a dance ticket, which was split between the girls and the dance hall owners. Some girls danced up to fifty times a night and made small fortunes from this arduous toil. They were often paid in small ivory discs, which they redeemed for cash or gold dust at the end of the night. But these "hurdy girls" also received a great deal of unwanted attention, and over a hundred of them met violent deaths at the hands of brutal dance partners.

As well as these more innocent pleasures, a thriving sex industry also grew in the West. It is estimated that at least 90 percent of the women in the mining camps were prostitutes. Many unprotected women, widows, and orphans were forced to turn to prostitution to support themselves, but others deliberately chose the profession. Some were looking for a nest egg to start a new life, while others sought a male protector. Others saw prostitution as a legitimate career in itself. As one Denver prostitute stated, "I went into the sporting life for business reasons and no other. It was a way for a woman in those days to make money and I made it."

Above: *Timberline, a noted Dodge City prostitute.*

In John Wayne's Western movies, several good-time girls meet the love of their lives in the course of their career as saloon girls, and begin a "normal" relationship. These include Angie Dickinson's character, Feathers, in Howard Hawks's 1959 film, *Rio Bravo*. She plays a leggy saloon girl who romances Wayne's character, Sheriff John T. Chance, and makes him fall in love with her. Despite her chosen career, Feathers is portrayed as a loyal and loving woman with great strength of character. She secretly watches over Chance while he sleeps, protecting him from his enemies.

"Sporting" girls provide the love interest in several other Wayne westerns. His *Stagecoach* character, Ringo, falls for Dallas the saloon girl, and treats her with the utmost respect, despite her sullied reputation. They end the film together. Even the misogynistic Sam McCord can't help himself falling for good time girl Angel in *North to Alaska* (1960).

Gold miners referred to "professional" women as "ladies of the line" or "sporting women," while cowboys called them "soiled doves." Other euphemisms included "daughters of sin," "fallen frails," "doves of the roost," "scarlet ladies," "nymphs du prairie," "fair belles," "fallen angels," and less gallantly, "painted cats."

As the trade developed, a hierarchical system of prostitution grew up. At the lowest level, single unprotected prostitutes worked the streets. These women were often alcoholics or drug addicts at the end of their careers. They carried blankets to bed down on the ground and plied their trade for a few coins, drink, or drugs. Slightly higher up the "professional" ladder were women who worked in the notorious "cribs." These were single, self-employed prostitutes working out of tiny, two-room apartments, which cost around $25 a week to rent. They charged between a quarter and two dollars for their services and entertained as many as sixty men each night. The forty-niners called streets made up of rows of cribs "the line." Sometimes, these women were on their way up in the profession and moved on to lower class brothels, or "cat houses." Women who stayed in the cribs had a life expectancy of only six years.

Brothels serviced a smaller and more affluent clientele and offered the girls a little more security and protection. The women in these establishments charged around $10 to $20 for a whole night of their time. Alternatively, the girls might set a ten-minute timer to entertain as many customers as possible.

At the top of the profession were the "parlor houses," and this was where the real money was made from prostitution. The "Madams" who ran these high-class brothels were often accomplished businesswomen and became both rich and notorious. They attracted the best looking and most accomplished girls to their establishments and protected them as best as they could. Parlor house prostitutes often became courtesans or mistresses, with their own particular clientele. Each had her own lavishly decorated bedroom, a large wardrobe of beautiful gowns and a trunk for her savings. These fancy prostitutes paid their Madams for board and lodging, in a kind of cooperative business arrangement. For their part, the Madams paid off the police, kept "house" discipline, and served the ladies' clients with fine food and drink.

The girls in these establishments charged around $20 to $30 for a night's company, but there were instances of girls being paid fabulous sums of money for their time. A generous gold miner gave prostitute Julia Bulette no less than $1,000 to spend the night with him. Prostitutes often hoped to return to a more "normal" way of life after a lucrative career and used colorful aliases to protect their identities, and the good name of their families. Dixie Lee was the most popular sobriquet for these "ladies of the lamp," but familiar nicknames also included "Sweet Marie," "Ping Pong," "Timberline," and "Caprice." The "Spanish Queen," "Mary," and "Diamond Lil" were also famous prostitutes.

Although it was very difficult for prostitutes to make a fortune in the business of vice, some were able to graduate to being "Madams." Many of these women became highly successful. One famous Madam, Pearl de Vere, was

Below: *Rose of Cimarron, a well-known prostitute associated with the Dalton Gang.*

reputed to charge her guests $250 per night at her exclusive establishment, "The Old Homestead," in Cripple Creek, Colorado. The notorious "Mammy Pleasant," also known as the "Lady of the Frontier," allegedly was the wealthiest woman in San Francisco. Other famous bordello proprietors included Fannie Porter of San Antonio, Dora DuFran of the Black Hills, Josephine Hensley of Montana, Mollie Johnson of Deadwood, and Laura Ziegler of Fort Smith, Arkansas. The first Oriental madam, Ah Toy, arrived in San Francisco in 1849. She coined the pidgin-English mantra, "Two bittee lookee, fo bittee feelee, six bittee doee."

Below: *Miss Laura's brothel in Fort Smith, Arkansas.*

In *The Spoilers* (1942), Marlene Dietrich's character, Cherry Malotte, is both a highly regarded saloon chanteuse and a business woman. She and her lover, Roy Glennister (John Wayne), have shared ownership in a gold mine, which gives us a good idea of how lucrative a saloon girl's career could be. The role of saloon singer had become iconic for Dietrich since her appearance as Frenchy in the 1939 movie, *Destry Rides Again,* playing against James Stewart. The role had effectively re-established her career, since being condemned as "box office poison" in the mid-1930s.

Several Western women from infamous criminal families also made their living in the sex trade. Pearl Starr, the daughter of the gun-slinging "Bandit Queen," Belle Starr, founded a successful bordello in Fort Smith, Arkansas, while Wyatt Earp's sister-in-law, Bessie Earp, became the most successful Madam in Wichita. Doc Holliday's hot-tempered girlfriend, "Big Nose" Kate, was also a notorious prostitute and, latterly, a brothel keeper.

Brothels soon became commonplace all over the West, springing up in every new frontier town. There was even a floating barge brothel on the Belle Fourche River, which flows through Wyoming and South Dakota. The first "professional women" arrived in Deadwood in July 1876, including the unattractive-sounding "Dirty Em" and "Madam Mustachio." As Whitey Rupp, the owner of Wichita's famous Keno House brothel, remarked, "The wages of sin are a darned sight better than the wages of virtue."

The stark reality was that the lives of most prostitutes were desperate and unhappy. Abuse and violence were commonplace, and many working women were kept as virtual sex slaves. Chinese, colored, and Indian women were particularly badly treated. Syphilis, consumption, and depression thrived among these fallen angels, and many turned to drugs and alcohol to ease their misery. The use of opium, laudanum, and morphine was common, and suicide virtually epidemic. Girls overdosed, shot themselves, swallowed strychnine, and used chloroform to end their pain. Early death became so commonplace that the life expectancy of a prostitute in the Old West has been estimated at around 23.1 years of age. Very few made it past thirty.

Despite this, prostitutes are now credited with an important role in the settling of the frontier. Without them, many of the men who came to the West to make their fortunes would certainly have retraced their steps. These brave girls also provided an invaluable nursing service to the mining camps, saving many men from cholera and smallpox, with very little thought for their own safety. Despite this, as more "respectable" women came west, frontier society became more critical of these "fallen women," as the new states gradually embraced the social mores of the East.

Above: *"Big Nose" Kate, Doc Holliday's some-time lover and business partner.*

Acknowledgments

The Publisher wishes to thank the following for their help in producing this book:

J. P. Bell, Fort Smith, Arkansas
Patrick F. Hogan, Rock Island Auction Co., Moline, Illinois
Kansas City Historical Society
The Buffalo Bill Historical Center, Cody, Wyoming
The National Archives, Washington, D.C.
Mike Mooney, Mooney Custom Knives
Jay Saldana, Jay's Knives
Andrew Howick, MPTV, Van Nuys, California